D1167818

"Abraham Kuyper famously said, 'There is not a human existence over which Christ, who is Sove̶r̶e̶i̶g̶n̶ ̶o̶v̶e̶r̶ ̶a̶l̶l̶,̶ ̶d̶o̶e̶s̶ ̶n̶o̶t̶ ̶s̶a̶y̶. In *The Story of Everything*, Jared Wilson has followed the biblical storyline to show that Kuyper was right. And he's done it in readable prose for a new generation. Everything matters to God. Let Wilson help you understand what this means for you!"

Josh Chatraw, Executive Director of the Center for Apologetics and Cultural Engagement, Liberty University

"*The Story of Everything* is one of the most accurately titled books I have ever read. Jared Wilson rightly diagnoses the desperately 'truncated vision' with which most of us live our daily lives, and *The Story of Everything* is just the needed tonic. Accessible, highly engaging, and humorous, this book brings home the overarching narrative flow of Scripture in a way that leaves the reader hungry for the happy ending yet also eager to get the most out of every page in between now and then. I have been waiting for years for someone to write this book!"

J. Alasdair Groves, Director of Counseling, CCEF New England

"If you need to hear some incredible news, read this book. It will change you. In his creative sovereignty, God's plan makes sense of all the incomprehensible events in the world. In *The Story of Everything*, Jared serves as a wise, caring, funny, and insightful tour guide who explores the terrain of this promise. When you feel the haunt of futility or if you ever feel lost, it is important to know that God has a plan for everything."

Justin S. Holcomb, Episcopal priest; professor, Gordon-Conwell Theological Seminary; author, *On the Grace of God*

"We serve a grand and glorious God who does indeed have a plan for this world. How do we fit into this plan? Dig in. Jared Wilson gives us a thought-provoking glimpse into the big questions of life and the greatest story of all—God's story."

Jacob Tamme, tight end for the Atlanta Falcons

"It's fitting that a book called *The Story of Everything* would weave together things like the cosmos and pets, Augustine and Plato, football and Ecclesiastes. In a truly accessible way, Jared Wilson helps us see that there is indeed something that links all this and more together."

Michael Kelley, Director of Groups Ministry, Lifeway Resources Division

"Imagine going on a trip without having any idea as to your destination. You would end up confused, lost, and probably pretty scared. Knowing the starting place and destination is a crucial part of every journey. Too many Christians end up confused, lost, and even scared because they don't know the beginning and end of the journey called 'life.' If you don't know what God is up to, it's hard to trust him when things seem out of control. In *The Story of Everything*, Jared Wilson uses the Bible as a map to take the reader from the beginning of time to the return of Christ. Wilson helps us see just what God is up to, in order that we might love God more, worship God, and live on earth as citizens of heaven."

Stephen Altrogge, author, *The Greener Grass Conspiracy* and *Untamable God*

"This book really made me think, well, about everything! Jared helped make sense of how my life and talents fit into God's story of grace and glory!"

Daniel Seavey, recording artist; 2015 *American Idol* finalist

"Like a tour of life, Wilson takes the story of the infinite grace and glory of God colliding with the souls of man and shows how it relates to bacon, to sex, to work—to everything. As a former athlete, current husband, father, pastor, author, and bacon-eater (of whom I am the foremost), I needed this guided tour of life, this story of everything, and the grace beyond the sun that makes it matter."

Jim Essian, Pastor, The Paradox Church; former professional baseball player; author, *Like Father, Like Sons*

"*The Story of Everything* is a small *summa* for our time. Wilson holds the multifaceted jewel of the world up to the light of the gospel, slowly rotating it, allowing the reader to see the present and future goodness of God reflecting and refracting in every part. Insightful, profound, simple, and witty. Wilson has the gift of writing with theological depth and precision while maintaining complete clarity and popular appeal."

Steve Bezner, Lead Pastor, Houston Northwest Church

"We humans have bad memories when it comes to God's redemptive work, which means we often don't realize how God's story of redemption impacts all of life—even the mundane parts. *The Story of Everything* reminds us that life should be lived differently because of God's goodness in creation and redemption. Don't miss this opportunity to (re)discover the wonder of the perfect God who has invited us into his story."

Russell L. Meek, Assistant Professor of Christian Studies, Louisiana College

"*The Story of Everything* is an engaging introduction to a comprehensive worldview where Christ is literally the center of everything and everything in life exists under his lordship. Wilson helps us see our place in history, live life in our present reality, and look forward to the blessed hope of Christ's return. The book offers a well-written, funny, and relentlessly biblical framework for all of life."

Bland Mason, Chapel leader to the Boston Red Sox

"Jared reminds us to joyfully live like there is a God who is good, powerful, and very much involved in this world. Cutting through the fog of our seemingly mundane, every-day lives, *The Story of Everything* trains our eyes to delight in this God who is at work to make all things new."

Erik Raymond, Senior Pastor, Emmaus Bible Church, Omaha, Nebraska

The Story of Everything

Other Crossway Books by Jared C. Wilson

Gospel Wakefulness

Gospel Deeps: Reveling in the Excellencies of Jesus

*The Pastor's Justification: Applying the Work of
   Christ in Your Life and Ministry*

Romans: A 12-Week Study

The Storytelling God: Seeing the Glory of Jesus in His Parables

The Wonder-Working God: Seeing the Glory of Jesus in His Miracles

The Story of Everything

How You, Your Pets, and the Swiss Alps
Fit into God's Plan for the World

Jared C. Wilson

OSAGE CITY PUBLIC LIBRARY
515 MAIN
OSAGE CITY, KS 66523

CROSSWAY

WHEATON, ILLINOIS

The Story of Everything: How You, Your Pets, and the Swiss Alps Fit into God's Plan for the World
Copyright © 2015 by Jared C. Wilson

Published by Crossway
  1300 Crescent Street
  Wheaton, Illinois 60187

All rights reserved. No part of this publication may be reproduced, stored in a retrieval system, or transmitted in any form by any means, electronic, mechanical, photocopy, recording, or otherwise, without the prior permission of the publisher, except as provided for by USA copyright law.

Cover image and design: Wayne Brezinka, Brezinka Design Co.

First printing 2015

Printed in the United States of America

Unless otherwise indicated, Scripture quotations are from the ESV® Bible (The Holy Bible, English Standard Version®), copyright © 2001 by Crossway, a publishing ministry of Good News Publishers. Used by permission. All rights reserved.

Scripture references marked NIV are taken from The Holy Bible, New International Version®, NIV®. Copyright © 1973, 1978, 1984, 2011 by Biblica, Inc.™ Used by permission. All rights reserved worldwide.

All emphases in Scripture quotations have been added by the author.

Trade paperback ISBN: 978-1-4335-4457-6
ePub ISBN: 978-1-4335-4460-6
PDF ISBN: 978-1-4335-4458-3
Mobipocket ISBN: 978-1-4335-4459-0

Library of Congress Cataloging-in-Publication Data
Wilson, Jared C., 1975–
  The story of everything : how you, your pets, and the Swiss Alps fit into God's plan for the world / Jared C. Wilson.
    pages cm.
  Includes bibliographical references and index.
  ISBN 978-1-4335-4457-6 (Trade paperback)
  ISBN 978-1-4335-4460-6 (ePub)
  ISBN 978-1-4335-4458-3 (PDF)
    1. Redemption—Biblical teaching. 2. Biblical cosmology. 3. Glory of God—Biblical teaching. I. Title.
BS680.S25W55   2015
234'.3—dc23   2014049264

Crossway is a publishing ministry of Good News Publishers.

VP   25   24   23   22   21   20   19   18   17   16   15
15   14   13   12   11   10   9   8   7   6   5   4   3   2   1

Contents

Conclusion

We always begin having made a conclusion. The story of my aching to know what on earth God was doing—I mean, what God was doing *on earth*—began with a rather startling conclusion about my place in the world.

I was roasting in bumper-to-bumper traffic on FM 1960 in Houston, Texas, one blazingly hot afternoon when I realized that I was an alien. The thought struck me as both out of nowhere and a long time coming, like an ungraspable part of my brain had suddenly become dislodged. I realized with stunning clarity, "I don't belong here."

Now, I was born in Texas and, save for three years of childhood spent in New Mexico, I grew up in Texas. But I never felt quite at home in Texas. And yet, the problem I had just found the solution to in that muggy traffic trap was not exactly about where I lived. It was more about the circumstances and my processing of them. It was about the thick traffic, sure. It was about the humid air, yes. It was a lot about the fact that at the time I was working three jobs *and* going to college. But it was mostly about the fact that I had no idea what any of my displacement meant. I was not just an alien in my culture; I was an alien in my own life.

This is what I mean: In all my routine—daily facing the grind of work-traffic-school-traffic-work-traffic-work—I felt completely lost. Like the proverbial hamster on a wheel. In that crucial moment of traffic-jam clarity, I realized life was happening to me and I had no clue what I was supposed to be working toward. It wasn't so much that I wanted to get out of Houston, although that was part of it. It was more that I wanted to know that whatever I was doing—wherever I was doing it—actually mattered.

I wasn't thinking primarily of being transported out of my life; I was thinking how great it might be if some kind of meaning were being transported *into* it.

I think this is largely true for everybody. Most of us can deal with less than dream jobs and staying put in one place for a long time if we can only get the sense that there is something important, fulfilling, and eternal about the ordinary stuff we do in our everyday lives.

Because isn't that what life normally is? Ordinary? Not many of us are international adventurers or ninja warriors. Most of us are just regular kinds of people. Most of our days look pretty much the same. Every now and then something out of the ordinary happens, both good things and bad things. They excite us or disrupt us, or both. We usually ponder the big questions of life in those extraordinary moments—at weddings and funerals, at the birth of a child or the loss of a job, when we win the lotto or have to declare bankruptcy. But hardly anybody is contemplating the meaning of life over their bowl of shredded wheat.

But that's what I did. Hands sticky on the steering wheel, classic rock blaring from my radio, sweat beading on my brow, I thought, "I was made for more." Not bigger. Not better. Not even different. But more. Deeper. Meaningful.

What if there was actually a key that unlocked all this stuff? What if there was that One Thing that made sense of everything? What if both mountain climbing and traffic jams communicate something beyond themselves when we discover that One Thing?

I've got that thing. It's in the pages of this book. It's in the sunshine and in the air and in the pop-up ads on the Internet and in the checkout line at the grocery store and in the roaring stands of the football stadium, and it's right there, actually, under your skin.

Underneath the crust of creation there echoes the beating heart of a promise made long, long ago. It is sending out a signal, tapping

OSAGE CITY PUBLIC LIBRARY
515 MAIN
OSAGE CITY, KS 66523

out a rhythm, informing us and reminding us that this world isn't all it's cracked up to be. What we certainly feel in our sorrows over suffering and injustice, and what we ruefully admit when we are honest about our joys and laughter, is that this can't be all there is.

And yet—the answer cannot be that all this means nothing. Right?

What even so many religious people, including their leaders, have missed for so long is that the very real God has a very real plan for this very real place. And it isn't just to wad it up and throw it into some cosmic wastebasket. No, back in the recesses of time, before time even began, God was proclaiming his vision for the world he hadn't yet made. And when he made the world, he made his vision clear. And while he didn't make the mess of brokenness we deal with every day in the world and in our own hearts, his vision is not so easily derailed.

The world is broken, yes, but God has a plan. And God's plan has always included making sense of all the incomprehensible events that disrupt our own.

God does, in fact, have a plan *for everything*. For sickness and health, for art and medicine, for marriages and families, for individuals and nations, for life and death, and for earth and creation. In the chapters ahead, I want to reveal to you that secret One Thing, the mystery God has hidden in plain sight everywhere. And I want to share with you the story God is telling through this mystery— how it leaves nothing under heaven untouched by heaven itself. We will spend quite a bit of time in the beginning of the big story (Genesis) and quite a bit at the end (Revelation), and then take a look here and there at how some curious dudes named Paul and Koheleth helped us make sense of the beginning and the end for all of us in the middle.

The secret makes every ordinary second bigger than it seems, including this very second right now. While you are reading this book, the future is having an impact on you.

So read on. Let me show you that God has a plan for everything.

OSAGE CITY PUBLIC LIBRARY
515 MAIN
OSAGE CITY, KS 66523

1

God's Modus Operandi

God's Plan

On August 15, 1977, a man named Jerry Ehman came across a radio signal from deep space that confounds scientists to this day. Ehman, a volunteer for SETI—an organization dedicated to the search for extraterrestrial intelligence—was monitoring the Big Ear radio telescope at Ohio State University. Looking over the printouts of what that Big Ear had been hearing, Ehman could see all the typical background noise of outer space: the standard movements of satellites, the signals emanating from earth refracted off of space debris, and the like. But then something stood out. There was an anomaly. A big one.

6EQUJ5. That was the sequence on the printout indicating a strong, unique signal from outer space. It did not match the background noise. In fact, it looked much like you'd expect a radio signal from an intelligent source to look. It came from the region in the sky where the constellation Sagittarius is found, and its frequency appeared to match the "hydrogen line," a promising trait for SETI researchers who figured intelligent beings might use the most common element in the universe to broadcast a signal.

Blown away by what he'd discovered, Ehman took a red pen and circled the 6EQUJ5 sequence on the printout, writing "Wow!" off to the side.

Scientists have never found the source of the Wow! signal. They have never heard it again, despite consistently listening in over the years to the same region of space with radio telescopes much more powerful than the Big Ear. They have so far heard nothing like it. And yet the Wow! signal continues to captivate, stirring curiosity and fueling hope that somewhere out there *someone* is listening to us, that someone is sending out a signal.

Why does the search for extraterrestrial life entertain us so much? Since the earliest days of UFO sightings and the burgeoning genre of science fiction in the likes of Jules Verne and H. G. Wells, what itch does yearning for outer space scratch?

One of my favorite movies is Steven Spielberg's *Close Encounters of the Third Kind.* Though overshadowed by Spielberg's other sci-fi masterwork—a little movie called *E.T. the Extraterrestrial*— *Close Encounters* follows similar themes but on a much larger scale. In *E.T.,* Spielberg uses the science fiction conceit really to speak to the ideas of fatherlessness and family. In *Close Encounters,* he speaks to man's universal search for meaning.

As the aliens get closer to revealing themselves to mankind's official spokespeople in a stunning climatic scene at Devil's Tower in Wyoming, key characters inexplicably find themselves making replicas of the tower or seeing visions of it. Richard Dreyfuss starts with his mashed potatoes at dinner. Eventually he's pulling up the landscaping to make a minitower in his living room. A little boy shares these compulsions. A scattered group is drawn together by their inner yearning for this extraterrestrial contact. It seems to speak to something missing in their lives, to promise an answer to everything that is unsettled in them.

When the aliens do finally arrive, for these aching souls it is like heaven has finally come to earth. Dreyfuss's character goes with them in their spaceship to lands unknown.

Of course, for many, many people, interest in science fiction and little green men and rockets to the moon aren't a reality at all. But I still think the inner human ache for the search for life in outer space is universal. We may seek to satisfy it in different ways, but we're all really trying to solve two fundamental human problems: loneliness and insignificance.

Deep down, though many do not realize it or admit it, human beings carry a deep-seated need to know and to be known, a need to feel *worthy*, to be part of something bigger, as if all that is around us is more than it seems. This is a collectively human problem, not just an individual one. We feel lonely as a species, not just as people, otherwise the community offerings all around us would do the trick. And being in community with people is extremely helpful and necessary. But our hearts still yearn for more. This is why we find it so hard sometimes to live with each other.

Humanity also faces the problem of insignificance. Consider how each generation, at least in the United States, identifies so strongly with cultural milestones like WWII or Woodstock. It isn't simply that we want to be thought great as individuals—though we do—but that we also want to be known as a great people. Tom Brokaw even wrote a book called *The Greatest Generation*. We identify strongly with our generations, our colleges, our states, and of course our nations. But these collective identities don't ultimately satisfy either. So what is the last frontier for man to be seen as great, to feel a part of something grand, universal, and important—not just in the world but in the universe? Well, outer space, of course.

Volunteers around the world today have set up their computers to take part in a vast SETI network, harnessing their collective strength to provide a great big listening grid aimed at the heavens. Every day these noble souls diligently scan computer screens and paper printouts looking for that next Wow!

But what is it, really, that they are looking for?

I think we are all really looking for connection and significance, and we're all looking for them in ways we can't quite get a grasp on with the ordinary stuff of earth.

But the good news is that the answer really is out there.

The Search for the Secret

When I was preparing to write my first book—a supernatural thriller involving the spirit world and scientific theories about hyperspace— I did a bit of reading about multiple dimensions and time travel. I was surprised to discover that some of these far-out speculations have grounding in the very real work of brilliant men like Albert Einstein and Stephen Hawking. One constant quest of these men is for the elusive "theory of everything."

I'm not really a "science-y" person, so a lot of what I read was really confusing to me, but I found the general ideas fascinating. The essential conundrum in the search is this: scientists subscribe to both quantum mechanics and general relativity and yet, as currently formulated, these two fields are incompatible. Enter in all the work of the theoretical physicists with offerings like string theory to help explain or reconcile the two. The so-called "unified field theory," or theory of everything, has taken on mythic status, like the search for El Dorado or the holy grail. The search has worn chalk and brains down to nubs. It is what gets physicists up in the morning and keeps them in the lab all night.

For the scientist, finding the theory of everything is finding the secret to the universe. It proposes to answer all the questions we have and reconcile all the disparate ideas, making everything unified and coherent and comprehensible. The secret once found will eliminate all the mysteries, satisfy all the longings, clarify all the misconceptions.

There once was a guy who called himself Koheleth who carried on his own search for the secret of the universe. He too looked for that theory of everything. He felt the inner pang of loneliness and insignificance and tried everything he could get his hands on to assuage it, even trying everything put together! He became the most educated, the most rich, the most famous, the most entertained, the most comfortable, and the most sexed man on the planet, but the secret remained. Koheleth writes, "I applied my heart to seek and to search out by wisdom all that is done under heaven" (Eccles. 1:13). He worked that chalk down to dust. He wore his brain and his stomach and his heart and his libido out. In the end, he decided this search is like chasing the wind. Why? Because, he writes, God "has put eternity into man's heart, yet so that he cannot find out what God has done from the beginning to the end" (3:11).

We've got outer space down in our souls.

Deuteronomy 29:29 says, "The secret things belong to the LORD our God." I suppose there are some things we will never figure out. There aren't enough chalkboards in the universe, not enough radio telescopes on the mountaintops to help us wrap our minds around some things. The finite can *look* at the infinite, but it can't rightly understand it. And yet, sometimes the infinite gives its secrets up. Sometimes God spills the beans, as it were.

One of the earliest Christian preachers emphatically declared, "But we impart a secret and hidden wisdom of God, which God decreed before the ages for our glory" (1 Cor. 2:7). For *our* glory? That seems to get at that "insignificance" problem. It makes sense that this glory would come from some kind of "secret and hidden wisdom"; we can't seem to figure it out on our own. In Colossians 1:26, the same preacher, the apostle Paul, said that the mystery hidden for ages and generations has now been revealed.

You reading this right now, lean in close; I have something to tell you. Are you listening? Okay, here goes:

That secret of the universe? I know what it is.

All right, I know that is an audacious claim. I've already confessed that I am not science-y. So where do I get off claiming to know the secret to the universe?

Well, I don't know the equation for the unified field theory. I don't know how quantum mechanics and general relativity may be reconciled. But that's all child's play compared to the stuff that really hits mankind's sweet spot. I do know the secret that fills that eternal void in the human heart. I do know what answers our longing for connection and significance.

Remember, it was Einstein who said, "God does not play dice with the universe."

No, he doesn't. But before we see what exactly God is doing with the universe, let's take a look at the games we *think* he is playing. To do that, we'll turn to the life of another historic figure, another German in fact.

Are You There, God? It's Me, Martin

Like Albert Einstein, Martin Luther was a tinkerer with ideas. The son of a copper mine owner, Martin grew up with high expectations to pursue a career in law. Dutifully working through a rigorous academic life with difficult studies in philosophy and logic, he often had difficulty reconciling his tutors' emphasis on reason with his own search for certainty. Even the law, Luther feared, could not provide a sense of security. It would seem from many of his recollections about his own youth and subsequent religious training, that Martin was a pretty neurotic guy. "If I could believe that God was not angry with me," he once said, "I would stand on my head for joy."[1]

The result of this confluence of expectations, education, and inner turmoil left Martin vacillating between the two poles of humanity: license and legalism. To some extent, Martin found himself given to his own appetites, but the guilt that resulted always plagued him. This guilt of course led him to a severe sense of religiosity. Caught between these irreconcilable differences, license and legalism—the quantum mechanics and general relativity of the spiritual life—he was disoriented and terrified. One night while riding home in a thunderstorm, as the story goes, a bolt of lightning

---

[1] Heiko A. Oberman, *Luther: Man between God and the Devil*, trans. Eileen Walliser-Schwarzbart (New York: Doubleday, 1992), 315.

struck nearby. In fright, Martin cried out, "St. Anne help me! I will become a monk."[2]

It seemed his sense of turmoil and his love for certainty had collided in that moment, and he was trying to make a deal with God to save his life. It was a deal he kept. Martin abandoned his aspirations of law and joined an Augustinian order of monks.

But where a life of ambition and money had not quelled his unsettled spirit, a life of religious devotion only seemed to make it worse. He wrote at one point:

> In the monastery, I did not think about women, money, or possessions; instead, my heart trembled and fidgeted about whether God would bestow His grace on me. . . . [I] could not but imagine that I had angered God, whom I in turn had to appease by doing good works.[3]

About the only thing that worried Martin more than his own uncertain status with God was what he saw as the Roman Catholic Church's exploitation of the poor and ignorant. It seemed to Martin that every sin earned a demerit with God and every good work a credit, but he could not figure out how to get his credits to outpace his demerits. Further still, he couldn't quite trust the institution allegedly ordained to sort out this merit system to provide the kind of comfort he sought.

Martin was caught. He was caught between a desire to be finally, eternally settled, and the realization that he could never reach that settledness, even with years upon years of religious duty and good works. In a way, seeking to "find himself" had brought him to the end of himself.

The apostle Paul, the guy with the secret mystery revealed, once came to a similar conclusion, writing, "I have the desire to do what is right, but not the ability to carry it out. For I do not do the good

---

[2] Roland Herbert Bainton, *Here I Stand: A Life of Martin Luther* (Nashville, TN: Abingdon, 1978), 18.
[3] Quoted in John Piper, *The Legacy of Sovereign Joy: God's Triumphant Grace in the Lives of Augustine, Luther, and Calvin* (Wheaton, IL: Crossway, 2000), 84.

I want, but the evil I do not want is what I keep on doing" (Rom. 7:18–19). Paul was caught too. The good he wanted to do perfectly, he couldn't do. The bad he wanted to avoid, he couldn't avoid.

According to Martin Luther's son, the escape from this trap between license and legalism came just as suddenly and blindingly as the lightning that drove him into the monastery.[4]

> In Rome there are a set of twenty-eight white marble steps called the Lateran staircase which, according to tradition once led to the palace of Pilate at Jerusalem and which therefore have been made sacred by the footsteps of Jesus. Throughout the history of the Catholic Church various indulgences (a forgiveness of sin or remission of punishment granted by the church) have been offered to devout pilgrims who ascend the steps after communion and confession. Many pilgrims ascend the steps on their knees hoping to attain forgiveness of sins. This is what Martin Luther was doing when he remembered Habakkuk 2:4!
>
> Luther's son wrote: "As he repeated his prayers on the Lateran staircase, the words of the Prophet Habakkuk came suddenly to his mind: 'The just shall live by faith.' Thereupon he ceased his prayers, returned to Wittenberg, and took this as the chief foundation of all his doctrine. . . . Luther himself said of this text, "Before those words broke upon my mind I hated God and was angry with him because not content with frightening us sinners by the law and by the miseries of life, he still further increased our torture by the gospel. But when, by the Spirit of God, I understood those words—'The just shall live by faith!' 'The just shall live by faith!'—then I felt born again like a new man; I entered through the open doors into the very Paradise of God."[5]

It was a lightning bolt of grace.

Suddenly, Martin had the answer. The unified field theory

---

[4] James Montgomery Boice, *The Minor Prophets: An Expositional Commentary*, vol. 2, *Micah–Malachi* (Grand Rapids, MI: Zondervan, 1986), 91–92.
[5] Ibid.

became fact, reconciling not license and legalism, really, but reconciling man with God.

And once he found the secret—really, once the secret found *him*—Martin saw how it began to impact everything within himself and in the world around him. The grace of God given freely to him in the good news of Jesus Christ received purely by faith provided the emergency exit out of the constant push-pull between God's commands and the world's temptations. God's grace provided the security Martin had always longed for. And it gave a resonance to life he could only hope for, seemingly in vain, all his days before.

There is an oft-told (but unverified) story about Martin meeting a cobbler who had recently converted to Christianity. Much like Martin in his youth, the cobbler wondered how he might please God with his new religious devotion. He asked Martin, "What should I do?" Perhaps, he thought, Martin would tell him to pursue formal religious education, seeking to enter vocational ministry. Instead, Martin said to the man, "Make good shoes, and sell them at fair prices."

See, like Martin before the lightning bolt of justification by faith struck him and like the cobbler with a desperate desire to please God, we all tend to think that God has set up the world to run along the track Christians might call "legalism." It is similar to what many non-Christians might call "karma." The idea is this: If you just put good stuff out there—positive vibes or what have you—if you just do good to others and have a good attitude, God (or the world) will reward you. The Bible does say, after all, that we reap what we sow.

The problem with this view of the world, though, is that we have so much evidence to the contrary. Bad people succeed all the time. And it doesn't take much time for people who regularly do good deeds to discover that they have not created a force field against injustice, sickness, or other kinds of hardship. Bad stuff happens to people who do good all the time. So if karma is the way the world is supposed to be running, it's not working out too well.

But in that way of thinking, it makes total sense that a shoe-maker recently converted to Christianity might think that there was another kind of job that would please God more than making shoes. Surely shoes don't rank too highly on God's priority scale.

Instead, Martin Luther discovered that "the righteous shall live by his faith" (Hab. 2:4), not by his works. This means two things. First, it means that real life, what the Bible calls "eternal life," comes not by working harder and doing more and being good, but by that grace of God we've been talking about. That's the good news. Second, Habakkuk 2:4 means that the righteous who've been made alive by faith (not by works) should then carry on their lives by their faith. So the cobbler could work every day on his shoes, secure in the fact that God loved him, approved of him, justified him, and secured him eternally *all because of Christ*, not because of his job.

But Habakkuk 2:4 also prompts us to believe this: making shoes can glorify God.

Grace is the secret of the universe.

And the reason grace is the secret of the universe is because it brings to creation the very thing that creation has been craving since everything went haywire.

God's Endgame

God's plan to bring lasting, satisfying connection and significance to mankind, to cure the angst for more that we all feel deep inside, to make us feel less like aliens and less like searching for them—is found in this thing the Bible calls *grace*. Grace is God's modus operandi in the world. Not everybody gets all the grace God has to give, but everybody who wants it does, and everybody else gets some grace just for being a human creature trying to get by in the world. (Christian theologians call this "common grace.")

What Martin Luther discovered is what we all discover: living our lives driven by appetites, seeking to gain as much pleasure or comfort or power as we can, does not solve the deep need for significance. It might medicate us against it for a while, but it just doesn't last. Alternatively, living on the religious duty treadmill, trying to earn credit with God through personal righteousness, basically just trying to be "good people," doesn't solve our deep need for connection.

But the signal is coming from deep space. It transmits on lots of frequencies, some stronger than others. God is doing something with us. He is meaning something with creation. The message of grace—unmerited favor—hits the universal need with a specific message. And it bids us turn our gaze to the heavens to see God's impressive strategy for the whole world. Your bank account is affected by this signal. Your weekend on the golf course is affected by this signal. Your family tree, your family holidays, your family dog—all are affected by this signal.

There is something coming through in this transmission of grace that affects everything, that *changes* everything. If we pan out and look at grace from the cosmological perspective, we see nothing less than the eternally expansive glory of God.

The problem of loneliness and insignificance is actually a lack of glory. The glory of God solves those problems (and a million others besides). It actually cracks the code of human existence and the future of creation. See, God has not been silent. He has declared these realities. He actually tells us what he's going to do with everything! Like a Wow! signal straight from heaven, Habakkuk 2:14 announces, "For the earth will be filled with the knowledge of the glory of the LORD as the waters cover the sea."

Habakkuk 2:14 explains the reasoning behind Habakkuk 2:4. The righteous are made alive by faith and go about their everyday lives by faith so that the earth will be saturated in the knowledge of the glory of God.

This is God's endgame for everything. Glory. He wants his glory to fill the earth, to drench it, really, making all the dry places alive again and all the dull places shine again.

This makes sense when we think about it, because God's glory is the *weightiness* of all that he is—the beautiful summation of all his attributes. And since God's glory is perfect and beautiful and, well, *glorious*, it makes sense that when we somehow receive that glory, we become more than what we already were. When creation itself somehow receives that glory, as in the vision cast by Habakkuk 2:14, it takes on the gleaming quality of perfection.

No place or thing is quarantined away from God's endgame. His plan affects everything. So God's vision for his glory has dramatic implications for both the people who receive his grace and the people who reject it. It has very real impact on good deeds done in faith and bad deeds done in rebellion. And it makes no distinctions between the sacred and the secular, the spiritual and the natural. God has a plan for dirt and flowers, for sports and video games, for sandwiches and milkshakes, for anything you can think of. His glory will be brought to bear on literally *everything*.

It is no wonder, then, that God is constantly talking about the priority of his glory throughout the Bible. He's been declaring the point of everything from the moment time began. When light first appeared, it came from the eternally preexisting glory of God. When man first appeared, he was made to "image" God's glory. When God saves his people from sin and their own stupidity, he frequently says he has done it "for my own name's sake."

Ultimately, everything exists for the glorification of God.

Some will say this makes God sound like a first-class narcissist. But that kind of objection fails to take into account two important truths. First, God is entirely perfect and thoroughly glorious. He is not like one of us dull creatures puffing up our feathers to seem more glorious than we really are. He is actually what he says he is, and he is not trying to prove himself to anybody. More importantly he wants to *show* himself. We would call a less-than-glorious person preoccupied with himself a narcissist or a less-than-perfect person claiming perfection a hypocrite, but God does not qualify for either of those categories. He is fully glorious and totally perfect, so we shouldn't begrudge his claiming so. But second, perhaps straighter to the point, God's prioritizing his own glory *helps* us. It is the thing we actually need! We don't have the glory that makes us feel totally connected and wholly significant, and we need it. The world is broken and is desperately in need of mending. If God's glory answers the deepest longings of the human heart, why would we fault him for talking himself up as often as he wants to?

Therefore, it's not for no reason that the theologians known as the Westminster divines decided that the purpose of mankind was to "glorify God and enjoy him forever." Mankind's joy is inextricably connected to God's glory. So in the end, what determines whether you are totally fulfilled and saved from ultimate despair is what you do with God's glory. Do you embrace it joyfully? Or do you resist it? The first option ends forever one's loneliness and insignificance. The second forever solidifies them.

The Secret of the Universe

So now you know the secret of the universe. The thing that makes sense of everything is the glory of God brought to bear by the grace of God. And God's modus operandi, his plan to reveal this secret, is the proclamation of the message the Bible calls "the gospel," the good news that the glorious God has sent the radiance of his glory to restore men who have sinned and fallen short of his glory (Rom. 3:23). As Martin Luther says, "For what is the Gospel but a declaring of the glory of God and his works?"[6]

When you connect these realities together, the constellation that results projects a picture of creation that gives meaning to everything. It is as if the reality we know is simply a pale version of some greater reality out there—or, rather, *in here*, at least somewhere.

When I was researching that novel about hyperspace and whatnot, I came across the theories about multiple dimensions. Basically, some scientists believe that at the moment our universe

---

[6] Martin Luther, "Psalm 22," in *Select Works of Martin Luther*, vol. 4, trans. Henry Cole (London: T. Bensley, 1826), 388.

began, in the event often referred to as "the big bang," our current four-dimensional world split off from a six-dimensional twin world. The brightest minds in the world use variations of string theory to explain how all this could be so. It is an attempt to reconcile some of the irreconcilable truths in the world of physics and quantum mechanics. More fanciful minds have used these super-string theories to speculate about the possibilities of using wormholes to travel through deep space or even back and forth through time.

I am not sure what to make of the science of hyperspace and the possibility of higher dimensions, but I will tell you I love the idea of children crawling through a wardrobe in our world into an entirely different one on the other side. I think it is one of the best illustrations of heaven that a mortal has come up with. My thinking goes like this:

If heaven is not rightly understood to be some place up in the sky or far away in outer space but more simply "the place where God is," and since God is omnipresent, would it not make some kind of sense to say that heaven is a higher dimension? This does not make it less real than our world or even less tangible, but perhaps even more so, though invisible to us now. And yet, what I know of this glory and grace and gospel stuff from the Bible is that God is seeking to make the invisible visible. He did this in a variety of ways throughout the Old Testament, peeling back the curtain between earth and heaven every now and again to give some frail creature a glimpse at the terrific glory behind, but he did it most decisively in coming himself in the person of Jesus Christ. God became man, and in doing so, the twin dimensions of heaven and earth got a little mixed up. It happened every time Jesus healed a leper or walked on water or raised the dead. It certainly happened after his crucifixion when he came back from the dead himself. And one of the first things Jesus did with those resurrected, glorified hands and mouth was eat breakfast (John 21:12). Surely nothing escapes the grasp of God's glory.

Since you now know the secret of the universe, you're ready to discover how this secret unlocks the meaning of everything. God is actually telling a story in the world about everything. But in order to see how God's endgame impacts our everyday life, we ought to consider how our everyday life fits into the story of life itself. What story is God telling with this glory, grace, and gospel stuff?

2

The Story God Is Telling

God's Plan for History

People who know me well know that the primary arena of my sanctification is the grocery store checkout line. There is no refiner's fire quite as hot for me as that one. It looks innocent enough. There are colorful magazine covers with amusing headlines to look at. There's candy. A sign overhead promises "Express Lane." But it's all a ruse. And I fall for it every time.

There I will stand in the twelve-items-or-less line with three or four items, waiting behind a person with what I can only assume is medically diagnosed "slow motion syndrome" and a cart full to the brim with tiny items with unreadable barcodes. Then that person wants to write a check, but he can't remember the date, his name, or how to write a check at all. So I fume. Oh, sure, outwardly I might look pleasant enough. But inwardly I am a raging storm of indignation. I want to grab the nearest bag of Corn Nuts and slay everyone like I'm Samson with a donkey's jawbone.

When I'm in my right mind, I think about what happens to me in this situation and I ask myself, "Why am I like that?" It's not like I'm transporting a kidney for transplant and I have to get to the hospital. I'm in a hurry, but for no particular reason except that *I'm in a hurry*. I find myself similarly agitated on the highway when stuck behind slow drivers. And yet, I'm also aggravated by fast drivers speeding by me "like they own the place."

Have you ever noticed that? People are always driving way too fast or way too slowly. Why is that?

Because you are the standard by which everyone should drive.

It's your world; everyone else is just living in it.

See, you and I tend to wake up each morning with the default belief that the world revolves around us. We're not consciously thinking that, of course, but we immediately begin our waking moments putting thought toward what we're going to do with "our day."

When I go to bed at night, I think, "What will *my day* look like tomorrow?" People request time, schedule appointments, present needs. They're all features in my day, supporting characters in the story of my life. I decide whether to be generous with my time with them or more discriminating. After all, I have a purpose for my time and my day and my week—*for my life*—and I have to figure out how everybody else fits into that purpose.

But of course, everyone else tends to do the same thing. Can you believe that? Me? A bit part in someone else's story? They think this is *their* life! I mean, how self-centered can you be?

The truth is, we all *are* incredibly self-centered, and the way we go about our days as if we're the star in our life story and everybody else are just supporting actors, props, or background noise reveals just how self-centered we are. If somebody dares to ask for too much, if somebody comes across too needy, if somebody infringes upon my day as if it's actually his—watch out. We don't like having our sovereignty compromised.

Fundamentally, we believe the story of our lives is actually about us. Our thoughts, our ambitions, our feelings become the motivating factors and primary themes of the story we are trying to play out. But then we keep finding ourselves dissatisfied, or even depressed or angry, because nobody else is acting like we're the center of the universe, least of all God.

It can be a scary proposition, but we ought to face the very real possibility that, whatever God is doing with the universe and as much as he loves us, we are not the main point.

Again, the problem is that we keep trying to write our own stories—with our work, our families, our gifts and talents and aspirations—but these stories cannot carry the quality of glory that we are hungry for until we submit them to the story God is telling. Until we understand the big, overarching story—what literary scholars call "the metanarrative"—of the universe, we will only be throwing our best personal narratives into the forgettable dustbin of history.

The metanarrative of God's plan for the world gives perspective and proportion to our own personal narratives, but it doesn't diminish them, really. If anything, placing our stories in subjection to the sovereign story of God enhances them, gives them more meaning and resonance. That's what's so great about the story God is telling. It makes sense of so much we find nonsensical in the world and it gives great importance to the ordinary things in our lives we tend to rate as unimportant or frivolous. What we discover is that, following the plot of Matthew 10:39, if we are willing to lose our storylines for God's sake, we will actually find them.

In another great twist, we discover that God tells stories differently than we would if we were on his throne. Most of us know what we plan to do and how we plan to do it, but we don't really know how it's all going to end up. We just hope for the best. But God declares the end from the beginning (Isa. 46:10). He may not exactly tell us what he's doing in the middle of his doing it, but we are not at a loss about knowing where we came from and how it's all going to end. In fact, what's really interesting about the story God tells is how it begins with the end in sight.

The Conclusion

Moses concluded that "in the beginning, God created the heavens and the earth." That's Genesis 1:1, and the story should start there, because if anything, it tells us that all this stuff we're working with was authored by God. He made it. There was a time when it wasn't—then, *poof!*, it was. All because he said so. When God tells a story, he isn't just blowing smoke. He's blowing entire worlds into existence. God says, "Universe," and the universe shows up. Only God could do that. But he's not just showing off.

As each stage of Genesis 1's account of creation unfolds, in fact, we see that God is going somewhere. Like the grain in a beam of wood, there is a grain to creation. More specifically, Genesis 1 establishes the direction God intends for mankind. We see it primarily in verse 28:

> And God blessed them. And God said to them, "Be fruitful and multiply and fill the earth and subdue it, and have dominion over the fish of the sea and over the birds of the heavens and over every living thing that moves on the earth."

So what is our purpose?

To enjoy God's blessings. To be fruitful and multiply and fill the earth and subdue it and have dominion over it. All of that basically boils down to this: Mankind is meant to enjoy God through engagement *with* him and reflection *of* him in creation.

That looks like a lot of things, including the building of civilization, the cultivating of order, the establishment of excellence, and the carrying on with intelligence. "Build things," God essentially says, "create things, organize things. Reflect me as Creator and Sustainer by creating and sustaining."

Now, if Genesis 1 is the big panoramic scene, Genesis 2 is the close-up. In Genesis 1, the Hebrew word for God used is *Elohim*, and in Genesis 2 it is *Yahweh-Elohim*, the personal name God later gives to Moses in the book of Exodus. So what we see in Genesis 2 is an intensely focused revelation of God's relationship with his creation and God's relationship with man. In Genesis 1 we see our place and role in the story God is telling. In Genesis 2 we begin to see some of our lines and plot points. As some actors might say to their director in an especially tricky scene, we ask, "What's my motivation?" If Genesis 1 outlined it, Genesis 2 fills it in.

Essentially, our motivation is glory. We don't have it, but we want it. It will answer our feelings of loneliness and insignificance. So how will we get it?

Every day we try living out our own self-centered stories, and the God-shaped hole in our souls doesn't get the least bit filled up. This irritating reality is constantly nagging, "You were made for more." So how do we decode this? How do we get an understanding of what it means to have eternity broadcasting from our insidest insides? How do we figure out what the "more" we've been created for *is*?

Well, we begin not with what we were made for but with the very fact that we were made in the first place. In other words, where do we get off thinking the universe revolves around us, when it existed before we did?

Genesis 1 and 2 remind us that with as much power and dominion as God gives to sinless Adam, there is still no mistaking who is in charge.

Who is in charge? The Creator: "Then the Lord God formed the man of dust from the ground and breathed into his nostrils the breath of life, and the man became a living creature" (Gen. 2:7).

Adam at this point had no sin, no corruption, no mortality. He had almost boundless freedom. He could apparently work without sweating, without getting tired, without getting hurt. He was immortal. But he wasn't God. He wasn't even *a* god. For all the strength and dominion Adam had—God had effectively given him a practical rule on the earth—he was still made of dirt. It was by God that he could even draw a breath.

This is the very first step in figuring out why you're on this planet and what you ought to do about it. Remember that you were made.

That Koheleth guy once said, "Remember also your Creator in the days of your youth, before the evil days come and the years draw near of which you will say, 'I have no pleasure in them'" (Eccles. 12:1). Why remember your Creator in the days of your youth? Because when you're young, you tend to be strong and fearless and stupid, and it is good to remember that you were created. God brought you into this world, and he can take you out.

Even the sinless Adam had this reminder:

> And the LORD God commanded the man, saying, "You may surely eat of every tree of the garden, but of the tree of the knowledge of good and evil you shall not eat, for in the day that you eat of it you shall surely die." (Gen. 2:16–17)

"God commanded the man." Even before he had any sin in him to restrain or to repent of, Adam had to obey God. Why? Because Adam was not God. He was made. And even that forbidden tree is a reminder of Adam's place in the world. Having given so much freedom, God says, "This one tree don't touch." The tree of the knowledge of good and evil becomes the visible reminder to Adam that he is not God.

Putting man in his place begins with remembering that man had a beginning.

But there's more. Man was created, yes, but amazingly enough, man was created *to live forever.*

When Genesis 2:7 tells us that God breathes into Adam the breath of life, as when Genesis 1:27 tells us that man is made in God's image, it reveals not just that man is alive but that man was given the kind of life God gives—eternal life. Immortal life. Death is not in the picture yet. It is sin that brings death into the world. But before that, the breath Adam and Eve are inhaling and exhaling is perfect, untainted by corruption or decay. This is God's original design for man—that he would live forever.

Genesis 2:17 says, "But of the tree of the knowledge of good and evil you shall not eat, for in the day that you eat of it you shall surely die." By this, God is saying, "If you *don't* eat of it, you will surely live." He's saying, "Keep your place, Adam, in relationship to Me. I am the Creator-Sovereign; you are the created servant. Maintaining this relationship means you will never die."

And yet we are still not seeing the full picture of mankind's position here. It's somewhat implicit, somewhat hidden between the lines—or more accurately, in the tone of the lines—but notice that Genesis 2:4 is a bit of poetry. It is similar to Genesis 1:27's poetic interpolation (and even to Gen. 2:23's poetry, where Adam reacts to seeing Eve for the first time). These poetic interludes are pauses to reflect on what is happening. God is doing all these great things in the historic chronology and then the text stops and breaks into a little song about it. Why? Because God is great and worthy of praise.

In Genesis 2:5 there is no rain yet. Why? It says the Lord God hadn't caused any.

In verse 7, who formed man? The Lord God did.

In verse 8, who planted the garden? The Lord God did.

In verse 9, who made every pleasant tree to spring up? The Lord God did.

In verse 15, who put Adam in the garden? "The LORD God took the man and put him in the garden."

I love that word picture because it conjures up a picture of God taking man by the scruff, like a mama dog with a puppy or a giant grasping a man by the jacket collar, and placing him over into safety. In verses 16–17, who is issuing commands? The Lord God is.

When we realize our place in existence—that we were made, that we are not God—the only appropriate response is to see ourselves in relation to our Creator and bend the knee, to deflect all praise and honor and glory to the Creator. With as much glory as God has given Adam here—again, remember, this is before sin—the active doer in this passage, the one making things happen, the one worthy of songs is Yahweh God, the Lord God. This is the sentiment reflected in Psalm 8:3–9:

When I look at your heavens, the work of your fingers,
    the moon and the stars, which you have set in place,
what is man that you are mindful of him,
    and the son of man that you care for him?
Yet you have made him a little lower than the heavenly
        beings
    and crowned him with glory and honor.
You have given him dominion over the works of your hands;
    you have put all things under his feet,
all sheep and oxen,
    and also the beasts of the field,
the birds of the heavens, and the fish of the sea,
    whatever passes along the paths of the seas.
O Lord, our Lord,
    how majestic is your name in all the earth!

Notice that the song speaks explicitly of man's glory and honor, but it concludes with a reflection on the glory of God.

You and I weren't made to celebrate ourselves. We weren't made to sing our own praises. We weren't made to act like we weren't made, like we somehow just spontaneously manifested out of our own self-contained awesomeness, like our own "personal potential" big bang. We were made from dust.

All hail the Maker of man from dirt, the Maker of dirt from nothing!

Man was created to live forever glorifying God.

We are getting closer and closer now to God's conclusion for mankind, what those Westminster divines called "the chief end of man." We were made, and we were made to live forever, and we were made to live forever glorifying God, and we were made to live forever glorifying God . . . and enjoying him!

Look over Genesis 2:8–12 and then imagine it with me in this alternate way:

And the Lord God built a warehouse in Eden, and there he
put the man whom he had formed in a cubicle to stare at a data

entry screen all day until he was sad that he was made to live forever. And out of the ground the LORD God made to spring up every tree that is gnarly and creepy and produces bitter fruit.

Maybe that actually sounds like your life! But God originally put man in a garden. And he filled that garden with beautiful vegetation—trees that are pleasant to the sight and good for food (Gen. 2:9). And all that land was surrounded by glorious rivers. And the richness of the whole place produced gold and other precious metals, resources for building and creating and expanding.

Look, human beings, you weren't created to be miserable. God made man glorious and gave him glory to enjoy.

We've been trying to get back to that glory and the enjoyment of it ever since. But we're missing the central principle, which is that God gave us all these good things by which to enjoy *him*.

So all of these things that he gave Adam to enjoy—before sin entered the picture—Adam enjoyed as a way of reflecting the glory of God and enjoying God's glory. God said, "I give you all of this to enjoy. It will make me happy to make you happy this way. But this one tree: don't eat it. You need this as a reminder in all your enjoyment that the joy comes from me. You aren't God; I am. So you need to recognize in your joy that there is a commanding Creator."

Let's go back to Koheleth, who said, "Rejoice, O young man, in your youth, and let your heart cheer you in the days of your youth. Walk in the ways of your heart and the sight of your eyes. But know that for all these things God will bring you into judgment" (Eccles. 11:9).

It almost sounds like, "Have fun. But not too much."

No, what Ecclesiastes 11:9 is saying—and what Genesis 2:4–17 is establishing—is the boundless joy that comes when we remember our place *and* the place of joy. Joy comes from God.

And since sin has entered the picture, we discover this by constantly searching for happiness, fulfillment, pleasure, and joy in things other than God. When we start treating God's gifts like they are Givers themselves, like the good things God gives us are themselves god-things, we miss out on all that we've been trying to achieve.

As Saint Augustine once said, "For Thou hast made us for Thyself and our hearts are restless till they rest in Thee."[1]

There's that eternity in the heart. We keep throwing created things in there, but created things had a beginning. That won't fit the shape of eternity. Only the eternal God will. So if you want real joy, real purpose, real fulfillment in life—the meaning of existence—you will turn to the living God who made you and who established you and who loves you and will say, "O LORD, our Lord, how majestic is your name in all the earth!" (Ps. 8:1).

So that's how the story begins: the main character (God) creates some supporting characters (Adam and Eve) and sets them loose in a beautiful setting to live forever glorifying him and enjoying him by taking dominion, subduing the earth, being fruitful, and multiplying, and God looks at what he's started and comes to the conclusion: "This is good" (Gen. 1:31).

But then it went bad.

The Crisis

Do you ever walk around your house noticing the dirty clothes on the floor, the toys scattered everywhere, the dirty dishes strewn about the common living areas, and think to yourself, "How did there come to be such chaos in the world?"

They're infringing on your sovereignty, aren't they?

Well, you're not alone. The reason your spouse can't "remember" to put their dirty underwear in the hamper is the same reason the NSA can't "remember" what it did with all those e-mails Congress came looking for. We live in a broken world.

Let's make it more personal. Let's hone in on your inner story, the narrative well-honed from rehearsal in your heart and in your imagination. Have you been a believer in Christ for a while and yet continue to wrestle with particular sinful thoughts or habits?

---

[1] Augustine, *Confessions*, trans. F. J. Sheed (Indianapolis, IN: Hackett, 2006), 3.

Maybe you ask yourself questions like, "Why am I like this?" or, "Why can't I stop doing this?" or, "Why aren't I more sanctified by now?"

Genesis 3 is the answer.

Genesis 3 chronicles the origin of the great crash of creation. It chronicles the origin of sin in the world, but it also gives us insight to its inner working. The doubts we embrace that take us into sin and the beliefs that keep us in it are all revealed in Genesis 3. This chapter explains why everything is hard and everybody's broken.

At the end of Genesis 2, Adam and Eve are naked and un-ashamed. Perfect life. Perfect intimacy. Perfect relationship with God and with each other. No sense of vulnerability, no secrets, nothing to hide, nothing to protect, nothing to be afraid of, nothing to justify. And then we turn the corner into the crisis.

> Now the serpent was more crafty than any other beast of the field that the LORD God had made.
>
> He said to the woman, "Did God actually say, 'You shall not eat of any tree in the garden?'" (Gen. 3:1)

Now, the Devil is not mentioned by name in this passage. But we know from later references that the Serpent is Satan (e.g., Rev. 12:9). It is clear, I think, that this is an actual snake and not simply a metaphorical reference to Satan showing up "in person," as it were, because in the next passage in the narrative, God consigns the Serpent itself (and thus, all serpent-kind) to slithering through the dust. So the most likely interpretation of what is happening here is that Satan is manipulating a snake.

But we may wonder, "When the Serpent speaks, why doesn't Eve say, 'A talking snake!'?"

It's possible that Eve isn't surprised by a talking snake simply because everything was new. She doesn't know "normal." (It's also possible that some animals before the fall actually had the ability to speak.) Not to mention that Adam and Eve are used to hearing the voice of God, and they are likely used to visitations from angels.

They do not have a view of the supernatural as foreign and quizzical but as natural and everyday. There has been no fall to make them skeptics or spiritually dull. So a snake talks, and they don't think, "Snakes don't talk!" They think, "Well of course an animal would talk in this wonderful, vivid, spiritually alive universe!"

And what Satan the Serpent says is fundamental to all the terrible things that happen next: "Did God actually say, 'You shall not eat of any tree in the garden'?"

Where God has planted trees of prosperity and glory, Satan has planted the seeds of doubt.

And now, every sin we engage in begins essentially with the question, "Did God actually say?" What's interesting, also, is that the name of God that Satan uses in the temptation is not Yahweh-Elohim—the Lord God—as was the case in Genesis 2, but simply Elohim, or "God." He is subtly removing that relational connection in his language. The very way he frames the question implies a distancing, a turning of God from the supreme Person to know to a theoretical idea to consider. (For this reason, Dietrich Bonhoeffer said, "Satan does not . . . fill us with hatred of God, but with foregetfullness of God."[2]) The way Satan talks about God is impersonal: "Did this quote-unquote 'God' actually say . . . ?"

But that's not what God actually said, and Eve knows it:

> And the woman said to the serpent, "We may eat of the fruit of the trees in the garden, but God said, 'You shall not eat of the fruit of the tree that is in the midst of the garden, neither shall you touch it, lest you die.'" (Gen. 3:2–3)

Now, we notice here that Eve has made a mistake right away. If we look back at Genesis 2:16–17, we see that God does not say they couldn't *touch* the tree's fruit, only that they couldn't eat the fruit. She has already added to God's word.

So we see not just the origin of the sin of denying what God has commanded but also the sin of *adding* to what God has said.

---

[2] Dietrich Bonhoeffer, *Temptation*, in *Creation and Fall: Temptation: Two Biblical Studies* (New York: Touchstone, 1997), 132.

(This will come into more importance later as we consider things like God's plan for art and sports and the like.) Eve has the basic gist, but she's already followed the trajectory of the Serpent's proposed story—basically, God is a great miser who wants to forbid you all joys.

"But the serpent said to the woman, 'You will not surely die'" (Gen. 3:4). Satan has now moved from planting seeds of doubt to direct contradiction of God's promised punishment. "For God knows that when you eat of it your eyes will be opened," he continues, "and you will be like God, knowing good and evil."

It's complex teasing out what is meant by "knowing good and evil." Adam and Eve already knew the difference between good and evil, not because there was already evil in the world or they had done evil things, but because the prospect of evil had been raised by God's commands. They knew from God's instructions what was right and what was wrong, what was allowed and what was forbidden. That they were perfectly obedient before this moment does not mean they did not know of the prospect of disobedience. They had free will. They had been choosing to obey freely. But they knew they had the option to disobey.

So Satan can't mean "they will know *of* evil."

When he says, "You will be like God, knowing good and evil," I think he's holding out the promise of an elevated knowledge, a place of authority and power that they do not have. God put them in the garden and gave them remarkable freedom. This tree is their regular reminder, though, that for all their freedom and authority, they are not God. So Satan is saying, "If you eat of this tree, you will have the kind of knowledge that God has that makes him God. You can be a sovereign knower."

This appeals to Adam and Eve. They'd been given all the connection and significance they could stand, but they decide they want more. They want the glory that was due God. So they take the forbidden fruit and eat.

The fallout is immediate. Genesis 3:7 says that they became

"knowers" all right, because they immediately realized they were naked and felt horribly exposed.

Isn't it interesting that the very first thing that happens after seeking to be like God is that they discover they are, in fact, very, very vulnerable? They don't feel empowered or enlightened. They feel ashamed. And so they try to cover up.

Crisis gives way to crisis. Adam and Eve do what we all do every day to hide our sin and brokenness and vulnerability: put on fig leaves. You might call it putting on a happy face or putting on your big boy pants or putting up a brave front. To one extreme, we adopt a swagger. To another, milquetoast passivity. The loneliness and insignificance we feel is a direct result of having reached for connection and significance beyond God, and now we all just try to play the right part to keep the ensuing shame and vulnerability at bay.

But then God shows up. He calls the newly sinful couple to account. What do you think they will do?

They do what we all do. Adam blames Eve, and in a way, God himself: "It's the woman you gave me." Eve blames the Serpent. My religion professor in college, M. B. Jackson, called this phenomenon "Blame Transference Syndrome" (BTS), and said this disease has been part of our fallen DNA since that first disobedience.

Understanding BTS helps us see how sin works and how infectious and complex it can be: We believe lies and enter into sin, and then we try to cover up our shame, dismiss it, hide from consequences, protect, and self-justify once inside sin's realm. Then, when we are called to account, we try to get out of the consequences for sin by offering some excuse about why it's not really our fault.

This is why everything in the world is so messed up. And it begs the question: How do we get out of this?

Well, we don't. We can't.

See, while sin is all our fault, it is nevertheless part of the story God is telling. When our firstborn, Macy, was about eight years old, she asked me why God made Adam and Eve if he knew they weren't going to obey him. It didn't make sense to her. She believes God knows everything, including the future. So why would he create them knowing they'd screw it all up? Why wouldn't he just create people he knew *wouldn't* screw up? Pretty profound questions for an eight-year-old.

I said to her, "I don't know why God does all that he does. Sometimes we can't know why God does some of the things he does, because he's God and the way his mind works is too confusing for us because we're not God. But I think the reason God made Adam and Eve knowing they would fall from glory is because he decided this version of the future was preferable to every other version of the future."

Macy thought about that for a minute, and then she asked the question she and all children have asked since time immemorial: "Why?"

"Well," I said, "think of it like this: God is writing a story with the world. You and I are a part of that story. Adam and Eve are a part of that story. For some reason, God decided that this story would be a better story than any other, mainly because this story gives him glory in a way that other stories wouldn't."

Macy remembered her first catechism questions, so I wasn't speaking an entirely foreign language here.

"Who made you?"

"God."

"What else did God make?"

"God made all things."

"Why did God make you and all things?"

"For his own glory."

We have to explain what it means for God to get glory. How does this story glorify God, especially since sin definitely does not glorify God? When Adam and Eve disobeyed, they were trying to steal glory from God.

But this is the part of the story called the crisis. It's not the end. It simply establishes the problem. It sets up the opportunity for the hero to be proven faithful and true, strong and courageous. And in the story God is telling, the crisis of sin sets the stage for the entrance of the glory of the rightful King.

The Climax

Nobody can tell a story like God. You and I couldn't have made this up. We *wouldn't* have made this up. Because while so much of mankind's artistry has copied the themes that come from the true story God is telling with the world, it could have originated only with him.

In the man-centered stories, the hero rises above adversity and conquers through the sheer force of his will—by fighting, by politicking, by being *better* than the crisis. In God's story, something extraordinary and unexpected happens. If you thought God making people he knew would try to put one over on him was strange enough, consider this: in the story God is telling, the next crucial plot point is that he sends his hero out to die.

And like a good storyteller, he's got the foreshadowing!

As God pronounces judgment on the sinners, he throws out this little line of poetry to the Serpent:

> I will put enmity between you and the woman,
>   and between your offspring and her offspring;
> he shall bruise your head,
>   and you shall bruise his heel. (Gen. 3:15)

Many theologians believe this is the first clue about the gospel. It's the first nod at the secret of the universe. It is very likely that in describing a moment where man crushes the Serpent's head while the Serpent is biting him, God is giving us a picture of the cross of Jesus Christ, where what looked like satanic triumph was actually messianic victory.

Then, after pronouncing judgment, God takes a look at Adam and Eve's feeble attempt at covering their shame with fig leaves and instead clothes them with animal skins (Gen. 3:21). He kills something to cover them. They had brought death into the world with their sin, and God is showing the seriousness of this by shedding blood. There is another foreshadow of the cross of Christ.

Like I said, you and I wouldn't have made this up. In fact, when we read through the many pages of the Old Testament, we keep seeing how even many of God's own people continue trying to write their own stories disconnected from the one he is telling about himself. Kings rise and fall, prophets come and go, nations seek power and get enslaved. The mighty men of bloodshed are celebrated, and the spoils go to the strong. The powerful are rewarded and revered, and the bloodthirsty are championed and lauded. Meanwhile, God keeps throwing little shepherd boys and farmers into the mix, subverting all our gluttonous glory-hounding with a constant, powerful reminder: we are not the heroes.

This vicious cycle of glory-hunting spills into the pages of the New Testament, where God's people live under Roman occupation and oppression. The land is theirs but not. The king is theirs but not. The situation has long grown beyond desperate. Some have simply accommodated to the pagan culture. Some have aligned with conspicuous religiosity. Some have banded together to foment violent rebellion. Everybody's seeking connection, everybody's seeking significance. And they're all seeking it as if they can write their way out of their own problems.

But then the real King shows up. And he comes not with swagger and a swinging sword. He comes lowly, riding a donkey. He washes feet, feeds the hungry, sits with sinners. He does all the things broken people think heroes shouldn't do but desperately hope heroes *would* do.

And the plot begins to turn. There is twist upon twist. It is almost as if, in the work and words of Jesus Christ, God is taking the story back to that garden. He does so in primarily three ways.

First, we see that Jesus endures the same temptations Eve and Adam did, but he demonstrates perfect obedience.

We need a perfect righteousness to cover us now that we're sinful and broken. Jesus has that perfect righteousness, and one way he manifests it is in undergoing the same temptation of Satan that Eve did. In Matthew 4, we find Jesus in the desert. He's actually in a worse state than Adam and Eve were in the garden physically because they were well-fed and healthy; Christ has been fasting for forty days and forty nights. Then Satan shows up. And so do the same three desires that tempted Eve!

Satan tells Jesus to turn the stones to bread, appealing to his appetite in the same way Eve saw that the fruit was good for food. Satan then tells Jesus to employ his access to angels, appealing to his deity in a way similar to how he tempted Eve to "be like God" (Gen. 3:5). Satan also shows Jesus the kingdoms of the world in all their glory, demonstrating their shiny appeal, echoing how Eve found the forbidden fruit "delightful to look at" (3:6). The DNA of sin we see in Genesis 3 is introduced here as some mutation to Jesus's perfection, and he rejects them all.

The narrative of Jesus's temptation in the context of the biblical storyline shows us the total redemption available to us through Jesus's work, not ours. Where Adam and Eve—and we—messed up, Jesus comes through. Where we failed, he succeeded. We are sinful through and through, so there is no sacrifice we can make that won't be tainted with our inability to perfectly withstand temptation. But as his temptation in the wilderness reveals, Jesus is sinless, so his sacrifice will be effective. Here, in a foreshadow of the cross, Jesus presents himself as a perfect withstander of temptation. "For we do not have a high priest who is unable to sympathize with our weaknesses," Hebrews 4:15 says, "but one who in every respect has been tempted as we are, yet without sin."

Second, Christ willingly accepts the blame Adam and Eve were trying to transfer.

Ever since the fall, you and I have been passing the buck, shifting the blame, justifying ourselves. Jesus says, "Okay, kids, pass the buck to me."

Adam says, "It's Eve," and Eve says, "It's the Serpent." In our own lives we are always trying to figure out who *else's* fault it is, and Jesus says, "Enough with all that. Give it to me."

The one guy who is without sin says, "Give me your sin. Pass the blame, the shame, the cover-ups onto me. I will take them." Jesus interrupts BTS by inserting himself into the cycle of blame and absorbing the accusations.

In the fulfillment of the ancient rite of the scapegoat, Jesus provides expiation by taking our sin upon himself, *as if it were his*, and taking it away into the void of nothingness at the cross. It is "for our sake he made him to be sin who knew no sin . . ." (2 Cor. 5:21).

But he does more than take away our sin. He gives us his perfect obedience. Second Corinthians 5:21 continues: "For our sake he made him to be sin who knew no sin, *so that in him we might become the righteousness of God.*"

So, finally, Christ transfers back to Adam (and to us) blessing, not accusation.

While Satan comes to accuse, Christ comes to accept. Where the law announces death, Christ announces eternal life. While we're all blame-shifting, Jesus is blessing-shifting.

When you think about it, the justice of the gospel is rather unjust toward us, because in the gospel Jesus calls guilty people innocent. And he *makes* them innocent. He doesn't just wipe the slate clean, he fills it with his sterling record of perfect obedience—we become "the righteousness of God."

When God comes to us that we might give an account, we start the defense presentation, and we start naming names. "I wouldn't be like this, if it weren't for my mother—she made me this way. I wouldn't act like this, if it weren't for my spouse—he pushes all my buttons. I wouldn't struggle with this anger, if my boss wasn't always riding me. I would be much further along spiritually, if it weren't for my pastor . . ."

The reckoning comes and we start naming names. But the name above all names, Isaiah 53 tells us, was willing to be named among the transgressors. He was willing to be called all kinds of names himself: friend of sinners, drunkard, blasphemer, servant of Beelzebub—the list goes on and on. But when that time for reckoning comes, he names us in a completely different way. He could tell the truth of the law: we are sinners, unholy, unclean, unworthy, accursed, dead. But he tells the better truth of the gospel: we are saints, holy, clean, worthy, blessed, alive. Amazingly enough, he is not ashamed to call us his brothers (Heb. 2:11).

Zechariah 2:8 reads, "For thus said the Lord of hosts . . . he who touches you touches the apple of his eye." This is where the phrase "apple of my eye" comes from. And this is a rather interesting phrase since it was a fruit in the eye that started this whole mess. But God is a jealous God. He desires to possess us for himself. And he has made his glory the point of human existence. So where our sin brings the curse of death, Christ brings the gift of life, that all who trust in him should be freed from the bondage of lies, shame, and passing the blame, and delivered back into the connection and significance we were designed to enjoy before the fall.

Jesus endures the temptation we cannot, he accepts the blame we deserve, and he transfers the blessings of his righteousness that we could never earn.

Praise God for the gift of his perfect Son Jesus, the only antidote to death! He has conquered sin in the climactic event of his own crucifixion.

But wait—there's more! The story is not over. In a way, it has just begun . . .

The Introduction

It is a bittersweet twist that the rightful King of glory should accomplish victory over sin and brokenness by dying. And if that were the end of the story, it would still be a great one, and yet incomplete. God has not created the world and allowed us to bring death and injustice into the place merely to forgive the trespasses. He actually means to *undo* them.

As Christ dies, the gears of history grind to a halt. The sky goes black. In the temple, where God's presence is said to dwell, the gigantic curtain keeping men out is shredded top to bottom. But not just so that men may go in. Now, the presence of God comes *out*.

The gears of history begin to crank in reverse. Time moves in a different direction.

Jesus comes out of his grave.

The witnesses stand in the garden. They expect death. They deserve death. But a new thing is beginning. God is reversing death.

When Jesus is resurrected, it is really, truly him. It is not an apparition, not a ghost. He is not merely resuscitated or recovered. He was dead. And now he's alive. His body is really his. And yet it is different. You can touch him. You can eat with him. You can recognize him. But then sometimes you can't. And he can walk through locked doors. He can ascend into heaven.

Jesus's resurrection body is his body, but better. It is tangible and yet glorified. "Thus it is written, 'The first man Adam became a living being'; the last Adam became a life-giving spirit" (1 Cor. 15:45).

At every step of the way of his ministry, Jesus has been proclaiming the in-breaking of God's kingdom, the manifest presence of God's sovereign glory. He is himself the presence of God's sovereign glory come to set everything back to rights. God made the world good, and we messed it up, and now God has come again in person to forgive, heal, and restore. He speaks in parables, little narrative glimpses into life in the kingdom, the way things ought to work when God's will is done on earth as it is in heaven. He performs miracles, providing windows into heaven itself, where there is no sickness, no fear, no death. And he proclaims the gospel of the kingdom and himself as King, so that all who would repent of their sins and believe in him would have the eternal kind of life they were meant to have before the crisis. If you want connection and significance, you can find it only in Christ.

And in Christ are found all the hopes and dreams we heap upon broken things in the world: the hopes we have for family and religion, for communities and nations, for science and culture, for sex and violence. All of the things we ask these to deliver though they can't—we find in Jesus. And this is why Jesus, as Lord over everything, gives meaning to everything. This is why God, who created everything, wants us to see everything in the world in the light of Jesus.

After his resurrection, Jesus spends some more time with his disciples, but he eventually goes back to that higher dimension we call heaven, the place where God is most manifestly known. The departed saints are there. The angels are there. The glory we still long for is there. And where it looks like the story should be winding down, it actually begins to pick up steam.

When Jesus ascends, the Holy Spirit descends, and we get this rollicking missionary adventure called The Acts of the Apostles, which chronicles the explosive launch and growth of Christ's church, which begins to face crises of its own in this sinful, unjust world. And while the apostles by the Holy Spirit seek to shepherd the early church to put their hope in the things of heaven instead of the stuff of earth, the whole big story ends with the promise of something entirely new. In the last book of the Bible, one of the apostles, a man named John, writes:

> Then I saw a new heaven and a new earth, for the first heaven and the first earth had passed away, and the sea was no more. And I saw the holy city, new Jerusalem, coming down out of heaven from God, prepared as a bride adorned for her husband. And I heard a loud voice from the throne saying, "Behold, the dwelling place of God is with man. He will dwell with them, and they will be his people, and God himself will be with them as their God. He will wipe away every tear from their eyes, and death shall be no more, neither shall there be mourning, nor crying, nor pain anymore, for the former things have passed away."
>
> And he who was seated on the throne said, "Behold, I am making all things new." Also he said, "Write this down, for these words are trustworthy and true." And he said to me, "It is done! I am the Alpha and the Omega, the beginning and the end. To the thirsty I will give from the spring of the water of life without payment. The one who conquers will have this heritage, and I will be his God and he will be my son." (Rev. 21:1–7)

So in a way, we are going back to the garden, before everything fell apart at man's disobedience. But we're not really going back. It's more like the garden is coming back. But this time it will be even better. All that we were meant to be and do the first time around is now infinitely possible under the sovereign glory of Jesus Christ who has redeemed sinners by his grace. We will be eternally connected to him and to each other and find our endless significance in being raised with him and exalted as his princes and princesses in the age to come.

The key, then, is to figure out how what's behind us and what's ahead of us impact what's all around us. It is that vision of a new "heavenly" earth—not really of an outer-space kind of disembodied heaven—that the New Testament writers keep holding out for the believers living in cultures of injustice, persecution, sickness, and death. The apostle Peter writes, "But according to his promise we are waiting for new heavens and a new earth in which righteousness dwells" (2 Pet. 3:13). That was the persecuted church's consolation. He didn't say, "Don't worry; one day you'll be vacuumed out of this world into an ethereal place of pure spirit." He is saying, "Don't worry; one day Jesus will return and vanquish sin and death permanently, and this world will become new again." And all the stuff we enjoy now from God—family, art, culture, sports, etc.—we will enjoy in new ways *with* God.

This is the story God is telling. I have plotted it in this chapter Conclusion, Crisis, Climax, and Introduction. (Some theologians plot it like this: Creation, Fall, Redemption, Restoration.) The story starts with a conclusion—"It was very good" (Gen. 1:31). And it ends with a beginning—"Behold, I am making all things new" (Rev. 21:5). And it's these bookends that help us see how the big story—the metanarrative of God's glory brought to bear in the gospel of grace—impacts all the little stories under heaven. Every character, every set, every prop—*everything*—has a place in the story God is telling.

And now the story really takes off . . .

3

Better Than Heaven

God's Plan for Creation

I was in a ninth-grade English class when I was startled awake by my first exposure to a non-Christian worldview propaganda. I mean, I knew it was out there, but growing up in the cloister of church culture and attending most of my childhood either a Christian school or a public school deep in the Bible Belt, I had yet to hear so nonchalant a shot across the bow of biblical history. But there I was in a public high school in Albuquerque, New Mexico, listening to my English teacher inform the class that every culture throughout history has had a flood story in their mythology and the story of Noah found in the Bible was just one variation among many alternate myths.

I sat up straight. I raised my hand.

My teacher sighed. "Yes?"

I asked, "Are you saying that the story of Noah and the flood in the Bible isn't true?"

"I'm saying," she said, "that every culture has come up with their own stories to explain the world around them and their place in it. So the stories are certainly 'true' for them."

"But that's not the same thing as saying it actually happened."

"Right," she said, and she went on to distinguish history from mythology. In the end, what she stressed was that since everybody had a flood myth, everybody was wrong.

But I had read plenty of C. S. Lewis by this point in my life, enough to know to come at this alleged predicament from another angle. I suggested that the opposite conclusion was just as likely, perhaps more likely. I said, "But if everyone has a flood story, wouldn't that be some indication that something actually happened? They can't all be right about the details, of course, if their details are all different. But wouldn't the fact that every culture has some story about a cataclysmic flood over the inhabitable world be more of an indication that such a thing might have happened than that it didn't?"

Where my teacher saw the discrepancies and therefore the falsehood, I saw the similarities and therefore knew there must be some truth to it.

Lewis had helped me with a few of his essays to see mythology not as some kind of rival or comparative religion to Christianity but as pale visions of the truth of Christianity. In his novel *Perelandra*, he calls myth "gleams of celestial strength and beauty falling on a jungle of filth and imbecility."[1] It's one of my favorite lines ever, and it lodged into my brain the moment I read it. I want to come back to this concept in chapter 5 about God's plan for culture (art, science, and work), but for now, I think it's important to point out that all the various religions and alternative philosophies and ancient (and new) mythologies aren't proof that nothing is true, but that something is.

The philosopher Plato told a parable about a cave, in which he said that the world around us is like the shadows cast on the cave walls from an unseen fire. The shadows are not the reality, but they are proof that there is a deeper reality, a deeper truth. Similarly, the myths we spin to make sense of the world, the idols we worship,

---

[1] C. S. Lewis, *Perelandra* (New York: Macmillan, 1965), 201.

and the ambitions we load down with the hopes of heaven are all flickering shadows on the cave wall.

Deep down, we all search for meaning, for beauty, for the honest-to-goodness Truth with a capital *T* that answers everything. And all the ancient myths, while not historically or factually true, at least give good evidence that there is some kind of Truth out there.

Christians of course believe that Truth is found in the story the Bible tells about God and his plan for the world. Lewis called Christianity, in fact, the "myth become fact." The Bible's story is true and not just in the sense that my ninth grade English teacher meant—"true for us." It is the real truth. It is true independent of belief or disbelief. It is the fire that casts the shadows in Plato's cave.

And one great reason to believe that the Bible's story is true despite its occasional similarities to other stories is because it is actually so different from other stories.

For instance, ancient peoples would have noticed right away how unique the Jews' creation story was compared to their own. And to this day if you go to native peoples and hear their creation myths, you will still see how utterly unique the Bible's truth about creation really is. In nearly all other origin stories, there are, first of all, multiple gods. For nearly every object, experience, and phenomena, there is a corresponding deity. The Jews came along and said, "Nope. Just one God." Well, that's different.

And then the way these other so-called gods go about making stuff is very crude. They make things through sex and violence with each other. I once studied the creation myths of the Yanomamo people of the Amazon rainforest when researching a novel. They believed the earth was formed when one god stabbed another god. The victim bled out and the blood formed the earth. This is not much different from some of the ancient creation stories in cultures around the world. But not the biblical creation story. There is one God, and he makes the world by simply speaking it into existence. No sex, no violence, no soap-operatic scheming in the heavens. Just God saying, "Let there be light."

What we find in Genesis 1 is certainly poetic. It reads similarly to the language and tone of other creation myths. And yet, it's different. It actually reads like a historical account. There is a chronology. Some scholars believe the right order of creation is found in Genesis 2, and Genesis 1 is a song or reflection where the order is not as important, but even if that's the case, the distinctiveness of Genesis 1 is undeniable.

And the orderliness of Genesis 1 might explain the embedded orderliness of creation in a way that pagan speculation about blood-formed earths and hot-tempered deities might not.

God is creating the cosmos in Genesis 1:1 and, I believe, clearing out the promised land for his children in the rest of the chapter, but he's also creating something else. Genesis 1 lays the foundation for the truth about God and all his ways. It tells us: Yes, there is a God. He is very powerful. He made you and he made everything. But it also shows us that anything we want to know about *anything* must in some way go back to Genesis 1 and 2.

Genesis 1 and 2 is an anchor, a foundation, a template for all that is good and orderly in the world. Genesis 1 and 2's creation accounts are the source of all good theology.

The Ten Commandments, for example, are sourced in Genesis 1 and 2 when they tell us not to have any other gods and when they tell us to rest from our works on the Sabbath.

When John introduces us to the truth about Jesus in John 1, he goes back to Genesis 1 to place the Son of God at the scene of creation.

In Acts 14, the people in Lystra believe Paul and Barnabas are gods. They say, "No, we're just men," and take their hearers back to Genesis 1.

When Paul is preaching in the Areopagus in Acts 17, letting the people know about their "unknown god," he goes back to Genesis 1.

When Jesus teaches about men and women and marriage, he goes back to Genesis 1 and 2.

When Paul teaches about men and women and marriage in 1 Corinthians 11, he goes back to Genesis 1 and 2.

When Paul teaches on gender roles in the church in 1 Timothy 2, he goes back to Genesis 1 and 2.

When Paul begins expounding the gospel in Romans 1, he goes back to Genesis 1 and 2.

When Paul teaches on creation's redemption in Romans 8, he goes back to Genesis 1 and 2.

When Paul teaches in 1 Corinthians 15 about the resurrection and restoration to come, he goes back to Genesis 1 and 2.

And in Revelation, as John is given visions of the new creation, the language he uses keeps going back to Genesis 1 and 2.

Genesis 1 and 2 are the foundation for the truth about God and about us and about the gospel. So when we contemplate what God is doing with creation, we have to go back to his intentions as expressed in Genesis 1 and 2. And when we do that, we begin to see how the story God is telling—conclusion, crisis, climax, introduction—may be applied to this big ball of dirt and water we live on.

A Finely Tuned World

Before the wheels come off the whole enterprise in Genesis 3, we see that what God has made of the world is very, very good. He has with all creation made a show of his holiness and beauty. The crown of his creation, of course, is man and woman, bearers of his image in the world he has made for them to cultivate and enjoy. But the very hum and buzz of creation itself is tuned to his image, as well. It declares his glory. It is well made and well ordered. The tides, the seasons, the climates all reflect God's good standard. The world is tuned to his greatness.

God doesn't make junk. Everything he makes is imbued and embedded with excellence. And intelligence!

Not too long ago scientists discovered that only a small percentage of human DNA was used for making proteins, so they figured the rest served no real purpose. They called it "junk DNA," assuming it had no function. Then a new project called ENCODE began to identify all the functional elements in the human gene code. Do you know what they discovered? Yes, only 1 percent of DNA codes for proteins, but 20 percent is biologically functional and 80 percent is biochemically functional. Suddenly that "junk DNA" didn't seem so junky. An Australian science reporter writes, "The old concept doesn't explain this. We have misunderstood the system for the last 50 years based on a incorrect assumption."[2]

Doctors used to believe that the human appendix served no purpose in the body. Then Duke Medical School researchers discovered that the appendix produces and protects good germs for the body and serves to reboot the digestive system.

The more we discover about creation and our created selves, the more intelligent design we find embedded there. This is an echo of God's goodness, that he's left his virtual fingerprints everywhere.

If Genesis 1 and 2 show us anything, it's how orderly God is, how much of a caretaker he is, how organized his standards are. So it makes sense that we'd see this order in things like the solar system—every planet and moon perfectly placed and balanced around each other and around the sun at the center to sustain human life here. And it makes sense that we'd see the fingerprints of this order all around us.

Have you ever heard of the Fibonacci sequence?

The Fibonacci sequence is the list of numbers where each is the sum of the two numbers before it. So you start with 0, obviously, and then the sequence runs 0, 1, 1, 2, 3, 5, 8, 13, 21, 34, and so on.

What's interesting about the Fibonacci sequence is that when you make squares with the widths of the numbers, it creates a spiral image. The "Fibonacci spiral" is found everywhere. It is found in plant leaves, pinecones, pineapples, daisies, and sunflowers. It's in the shell of the nautilus. It's in starfish. It's in the cochlea of your inner ear. I don't mean simply a spiraled shape. I mean the actual

2 "ENCODE Reveals Junk DNA Not Junk after All," *The Science Show* online, October 20, 2012, http://www.abc.net.au/radionational/programs/scienceshow/encode-reveals-junk-dna-not-junk-after-all/4323436/.

Fibonacci spiral, with the proportions corresponding to the Fibonacci number sequence.

God has embedded order, intelligence, and design into his creation. It's not just the heavens that declare the glory of God, it's the discarded seashells!

The birds and butterflies know where to go at their appointed times in the year. The tides and the jet stream follow their prescribed courses. The planets keep their orbits and my dog circles twice before curling up in his bed. The sun keeps coming up.

What God has made is finely tuned. It was originally tuned to his own sustaining glory. But in giving man dominion over this fantastic creation, God was anticipating a twist in his own story. And it begins with creation getting thrown out of whack by the very ones who were made its caretakers.

Creation's Curse

One day I was having lunch with my wife at a local Italian café and the proprietors had the peculiar notion to tune the overhead television to a nature channel. While I ate my delicious sausage and olive calzone, geologists recounted the events leading up to the 1980 eruption of the volcano Mount St. Helens in Washington State. That eruption was the biggest in United States history and killed fifty-seven people. It was an interesting contrast, I must tell you, noshing on one of God's delicious creations while being entertained with the reality that God's creation could turn on me at any second.

Skiers enjoy the cascading snow of their favorite mountains, and then an avalanche strikes. Surfers shoot the curls off their favorite beaches, a wrong fall away from killer waves or coral or sharks. Every day we open up the newspaper to discover which beloved food is the new hidden danger. Is it eggs? Coffee? Gluten?

What was it like, I wonder, to make that transition from a world of pure wonder and beauty and security into the world still wondrous and beautiful but now . . . dangerous? In one second, Adam and Eve had the run of the place, and in the very next the place was running them.

In another interesting twist to the story God is telling, we learn that it's not just the characters who fall when sin enters the play—the entire stage does too. Creation, as a result of man's disobedience, has itself fallen short of the glory of God.

We see it right away in the curse God pronounces in response to Adam's disobedience:

The LORD God said to the serpent,

"Because you have done this,
    cursed are you above all livestock
    and above all beasts of the field;
on your belly you shall go,
    and dust you shall eat
    all the days of your life." (Gen. 3:14)

In a way, God is punishing all snakes for the sin of the Devil. That seems a little harsh, but it is an integral part of the story of his glory that God is telling with creation itself. Sin is a terrible thing. It is an act of rebellion, of treason. So as a reminder of just how terrible sin is, the consequences must be just as terrible.

We don't know if snakes had legs before this moment, if God in this curse is taking them away. Perhaps more likely is that God is now declaring why serpents did not have legs from the beginning, in a similar way that God declares the purpose of the rainbow after the great flood, even though rainbows had undoubtedly been seen before.

But lest we think this punishment is too harsh for animals, we must remember that first of all, God owns them. He may do with animals what he wishes. And cursing them in various ways is another way to enhance the terrible consequences for mankind in response to their sins. Why are mules so stubborn? Why are cats so smug? Why do great white sharks eat us? Because our sin has created a great disharmony not just between us and God but within creation itself.

We even see in some of the laws in Leviticus that if an animal is involved in a crime or even an accidental death, there are consequences for the animals themselves. Not because they are somehow culpable or conscious of their role, but because their own participation in the fallenness of creation is not without the terrible consequences of that fallenness.

And it's not just creatures that are part of this fallenness but the very earth itself. God continues in the pronouncement of the curse:

And to Adam he said,

> "Because you have listened to the voice of your wife
>   and have eaten of the tree
> of which I commanded you,
>   'You shall not eat of it,'
> cursed is the ground because of you;
>   in pain you shall eat of it all the days of your life;
> thorns and thistles it shall bring forth for you;
>   and you shall eat the plants of the field."
>   (Gen. 3:17–18)

The very ground is now cursed. Thus deadly volcanoes and hurricanes and tsunamis.

The perfect peace of life before sin, the great harmony between God and man and creation—what is often called *shalom*—has been fractured. So in Romans 8:22–23, Paul says, "For we know that the whole creation has been groaning together in the pains of childbirth until now. And not only the creation, but we ourselves . . ."

Earlier he says, "The creation was subjected to futility" (8:20). Thus the pains and terrors of life on earth.

> I will surely multiply your pain in childbearing;
>   in pain you shall bring forth children. . . .

> By the sweat of your face
>   you shall eat bread,

till you return to the ground,
    for out of it you were taken;
for you are dust,
    and to dust you shall return. (Gen. 3:16, 19)

All of the work that once was full of strength and joy has now become hard.

Yes, because of sin, life is hard. And then you die. The immortality of perfection has now been interrupted; it has expired. As Romans 6:23 reminds us, "The wages of sin is death."

So if we review the fallout up to this point, we see that because Adam and Eve have rebelled against God, they must now seek to take dominion over a creation that is rebelling against them. They feel pain now. They get old now. They die now. Work is hard now, sweaty and slow going. Plants have thorns and thistles, animals have minds of their own, children cause grief. And then making all matters worse, the curse pronounces a deep sense of alienation and exile in mankind. It begins here:

> Therefore the LORD God sent him out from the garden of Eden to work the ground from which he was taken. He drove out the man, and at the east of the garden of Eden he placed the cherubim and a flaming sword that turned every way to guard the way to the tree of life. (Gen. 3:23–24)

The curse separates us from God because sin separates us from God. And this is the most devastating part of the curse. That perfect fellowship Adam and Eve enjoyed with Yahweh God is now broken. There is a divide between them. Because of their sin, God must cast them out. They dwelled rapturously, pleasantly in the presence of the glorious Most High in perfect accord with him, with access, with approval, with embrace in the garden of delights. And now they must be sent away into the wilderness.

We've been tuning our hearts to the spiritual SETI program ever since.

You get some of the angst of this sense of alienation in the world in the psalms. In Psalm 27, for instance, David feels surrounded, bombarded, and laid low, and he sings:

> One thing have I asked of the LORD,
>   that will I seek after:
> that I may dwell in the house of the LORD
>   all the days of my life,
> to gaze upon the beauty of the LORD
>   and to inquire in his temple. (v. 4)

Or in Psalm 51:

> Create in me a clean heart, O God,
>   and renew a right spirit within me.
> Cast me not away from your presence,
>   and take not your Holy Spirit from me.
> Restore to me the joy of your salvation,
>   and uphold me with a willing spirit. (vv. 10–12)

These are not just spiritual cries for help, though they are spiritual fundamentally of course. They are cries for actual, tangible, real connection with God. When David says he wants to dwell in the Lord's temple and gaze upon his beauty, and when he says he wants to be in the presence of the Spirit and have his joy back, he is longing for that day when all creation is restored under the presence of God's glory, when the shalom of earth is restored.

Now we see how far-reaching the curse is, and why Paul would say "all creation is groaning for redemption."

On Hell and Handbaskets

Well, then, what is God's plan for all this? We've messed it up. It's all broken. Everything, top to bottom. What now?

Is God just going to throw the whole thing out? Are we, as so many of our cultural spokespeople (appointed and unappointed) suggest, going to hell in a handbasket?

It would appear so from some Bible verses. Consider this from the apostle Peter: "But by the same word the heavens and earth that now exist are stored up for fire" (2 Pet. 3:7). Some think the world is so screwed up that God almost has no choice but to chuck the whole thing into the wastebasket of the cosmos.

When I was growing up, my church projected the end times in a decidedly cynical way. The world is going to hell, we were told, so things are going to get worse and worse until finally God gets so sick of it all that he takes his believers up into heaven before he destroys the whole place. In a way, this seems to follow the story of the great flood—God protecting his few followers from the widespread cataclysm he sends as judgment. But when the waters receded, Noah and his family weren't in an entirely different world, just a baptized one.

Similarly, evangelicals seem to talk about going to heaven as if it's the end of the story. God will get so fed up with how things are going on earth, this story goes, that he will finally evacuate his believers up into the ark of the heavenly space and send the flood of his judgment to wipe everything else out, and then we will spend eternity floating around with him on the golden streets somewhere in outer space. This is the truncated vision we get in the sentimental spiritualities of cultural phenomena like *Heaven Is for Real* or *Left Behind*. But these narratives, even when they find alignment with biblical truth, are only a part of the true story. They are gleams of celestial beauty but not the fullness.

No, we are not so powerful as to overturn God's creation forever. We are not so central that what we make of this world is what will finally be made of the world. Instead, God's plan of salvation, which restores sinners who trust in Jesus into spiritual relationship with him, also includes restoring them into the shalom that was lost at the fall. And this means that earth is not going to hell in a handbasket. In fact, it means that heaven is coming to earth.

Consider the following.

In 1 Corinthians 15, as Paul is rehearsing all the wonderful things Jesus Christ's bodily resurrection means, he includes the bodily resurrection of those who have trusted in Jesus for forgiveness of sins. They too will be raised to new life in glorified bodies.

In the book of Job, as the afflicted protagonist is lamenting the loss of everything in his life, including his children, his money, and his own health and life, he says something rather interesting: "And after my skin has been thus destroyed, yet in my flesh I shall see God" (19:26). He says, "I know that my Redeemer lives, and at the last he will stand upon"—what?—"the earth" (19:25).

Remember what we established as God's endgame for the universe? Habakkuk 2:14. His glory is meant to cover the entire earth, to bathe it all in the shining splendor of his own beauty and wonderfulness.

Remember what Jesus says at the end of the biblical story, when the narrative is really taking off? "I am making all things new."

If we consider Peter's words in context, we see more of the dire "hell in a handbasket" prognostication, but we also see the final hope.

> But the day of the Lord will come like a thief, and then the heavens will pass away with a roar, and the heavenly bodies will be burned up and dissolved, and the earth and the works that are done on it will be exposed.
>
> Since all these things are thus to be dissolved, what sort of people ought you to be in lives of holiness and godliness, waiting for and hastening the coming of the day of God, because of which the heavens will be set on fire and dissolved, and the heavenly bodies will melt as they burn! But according to his promise we are waiting for new heavens and a new earth in which righteousness dwells. (2 Pet. 3:10–13)

God's not throwing this place away. He's going to restore it.

An Earth More Beautiful Than Beautiful

Every summer for the last several years, my family has spent our summer vacation in Stonington, Maine. We like Stonington because you get that salty air and the crashing Atlantic waves and the delectable lobster without all the hustle and bustle of the touristy beach towns of Maine. There are some touristy things in the area, but Stonington is more of a sleepy fisherman's village. We like that we can slow down, breathe, and spend lots of time doing absolutely nothing but looking at the sky and the big ocean.

Stonington is on Penobscot Bay, and what's great about where we stay is that from one particular vantage point at Sand Beach, which juts out and faces the bay *westward*, you can actually watch the sun set over the water! Not an expected sight on the East Coast, to be sure. My wife has taken a picture of the sunset over the water from Sand Beach, and it's one of the most beautiful things I've ever seen.

When we're in Stonington, some friends who live nearby often take us out on their boat. We get to see the lovely islands in the area and watch the sea lions basking on the rocks. I like looking down into the gray depths of the ocean, pondering what scary and wonderful things lurk beneath the waves. It was this coastline that inspired perhaps the greatest American novel, *Moby Dick*. In Stonington, for me anyway, it is difficult not to think the world is beautiful. Even the sight of tired lobstermen hauling in their catches, hands raw from the salty water and clothes dirty with sand and grease, has a beauty to it, a glory.

I have not traveled as extensively as I'd like, but I've seen both jungles and deserts. I've seen oceans and landlocked plains. I've seen big cities and tiny villages. And I've seen glory everywhere. I've smelled the hay and the manure inside a Vermonter's old barn and felt the world was beautiful. And I've craned my neck to look up at the Empire State Building and felt the world was beautiful.

I confess it is difficult for me to imagine how the world could get much more beautiful.

We are all stirred by different things. I prefer the mossy forests of Vermont and the Pacific Northwest to the piney woods of Texas, but others feel differently. I prefer the foggy coastlines of New England to the sunny shores of Florida, but college students aren't flocking to Massachusetts for spring break. I prefer the mountains to the plains. But nobody can deny that wherever you go in God's creation, you are bound to find beauty.

What will this stuff look like, I wonder, when God restores it?

The damp woods around our New England home seem magical to me now. Will they be full of talking fauns in the world to come? Will the surging depths of the Atlantic become more glorious and yet entice me to walk on them? Will the sun-baked sand on the beach not get hot? Will the oasis mirages in the desert become reality?

From the beginning of time, we have looked at the world around us with both wonder and fear. One beautiful autumn day my wife and I hiked up to a high ledge called Deer Leap overlooking the Shelburne Pass on the Appalachian Trail. When we got to the top, she casually mounted the rocky ledge to look over the valley below, unnerved not a bit by the sheer face descending down the other side. I on the other hand crawled on my belly halfway up the slope and peered over. Where she saw adventure, I saw danger.

I think of some of the greatest wonders of the natural world, places that give some vibrancy and others vertigo. Think of the Swiss Alps. These towering testimonies to the majesty of God have been the backdrop for some of literature's finest and varied stories, from the sweetness of *Heidi* to the horrors of *Frankenstein*. The Alps are the source of poetic transcendence in Oliver Goldsmith's *The Traveller* and seductive danger in Ernest Hemingway's *A Farewell to Arms*. In *Women in Love*, D. H. Lawrence describes the beautiful quiet of the Alps as the doorway to danger this way: "It was a silence and a sheer whiteness exhilarating to madness. But the perfect silence was most terrifying, isolating the soul, surrounding the heart with frozen air."[3]

Where some feel exhilarated, others feel exile. It is difficult to feel ambivalent about a place like the Swiss Alps. And I wonder . . . their gleaming peaks are alive now with the purest white and are tall enough to scrape the pearly gates of heaven it would seem,

---

[3] D. H. Lawrence, *Women in Love* (New York: Dover, 2003), 335.

but what will they look like on that day when heaven's glory itself lights them up?

Because that's what's going to happen, you know.

For behold, I create new heavens
    and a new earth,
and the former things shall not be remembered
    or come into mind.
But be glad and rejoice forever
    in that which I create;
for behold, I create Jerusalem to be a joy,
    and her people to be a gladness.
I will rejoice in Jerusalem
    and be glad in my people;
no more shall be heard in it the sound of weeping
    and the cry of distress. (Isa. 65:17–19)

This is the forecast for creation held out by God through the prophets. It gives shape to the glimmers of hope found in God's covenant promise of the land to Abraham (Gen. 13:15) and in the last-days expectations of Job.

It turns out that when Jesus Christ came to earth the first time, he was ushering in the kingdom of God, what I like to call the manifest presence of God's sovereignty. He was showing us a bit at a time then what it looks like for God's kingdom to come and God's will to be done on earth as it is in heaven. This is what connects Christ's parables and his miracles; it's the common denominator between his healing of the blind and his calming of the storm. When God's reign brings restoration to creation, there is no more blindness and there is no more dangerous weather.

But of course we still await the fullness of God's kingdom. It has come; it is "at hand." But it is also still coming and still to come. So when Christ returns again, he will finish what he began in his first coming, consummating the kingdom of God on earth. At that time, he will bring with him the glory of a new heavens and a new earth. This is the vision the New Testament prophet sees of that day:

Then I saw a new heaven and a new earth, for the first heaven and the first earth had passed away, and the sea was no more. And I saw the holy city, new Jerusalem, coming down out of heaven from God, prepared as a bride adorned for her husband. And I heard a loud voice from the throne saying, "Behold, the dwelling place of God is with man. He will dwell with them, and they will be his people, and God himself will be with them as their God. He will wipe away every tear from their eyes, and death shall be no more, neither shall there be mourning, nor crying, nor pain anymore, for the former things have passed away." (Rev. 21:1–4)

The visionary is then taken by God's Spirit to a very high mountain (21:10) where he is given a view of God's restoration of civilization coming down out of heaven. He describes it as more beautiful than every precious gem on earth combined. It is the best and brightest of cultivated creation combined *and glorified*. He writes:

And the city has no need of sun or moon to shine on it, for the glory of God gives it light, and its lamp is the Lamb. By its light will the nations walk, and the kings of the earth will bring their glory into it, and its gates will never be shut by day—and there will be no night there. (Rev. 21:23–25)

Theologians debate whether this text actually means there will be no nighttime in the new earth. More likely this means that there will be no "darkness," as in nothing to fear. It is just as likely that when the prophet says we will have no need for the sun or moon, he doesn't mean that we won't have the sun or the moon. Rather, he means that Christ's radiance is the true brightness of creation. His glory illuminates everything. Everything false, detestable, fallen, and spiritually dark will be vanquished forever, and the glory of God will give the new earth a beautiful sheen that makes the sunlight on the Swiss Alps today look like the mashed potatoes under the heat lamp down at the KFC.

But, see, this is the hope the Bible holds out for fallen creatures in a fallen creation—not that we'll all get beamed up into a disembodied heaven before the earth gets blown up, but that we'll all get decked out in glorified bodies to inhabit the restored earth, which will be even more beautiful, more majestic, more glorious than it is now. And since we know by the Bible's promises that this is God's plan for creation, we've got a better sense of how to think about creation than if we thought it was all going to hell in that proverbial handbasket.

So the mandate for Christians now is to see the earth around us in light of the heaven that's coming. This has huge implications for *everything*—for the Swiss Alps and for your front yard, for the people at your church and for your daughter's goldfish.

All Dogs Go to Heaven

There's an interesting turn in Isaiah's forecast of the new heavens and the new earth. Turns out, it's not just about having a more beautiful earth and enjoying it without fear or pain or death. It's actually got some hope for that creature who keeps pooping on your living room floor. And I mean the four-legged creature, not your toddler. (Although there's hope for him too.)

> "The wolf and the lamb shall graze together;
>   the lion shall eat straw like the ox,
>   and dust shall be the serpent's food.
> They shall not hurt or destroy
>   in all my holy mountain,"
> says the Lord. (Isa. 65:25)

Now, this is poetry, so it's a metaphor for the peace that will exist in every sphere of life in the restored creation. But the implications are very real for our furry and feathered friends. There will be lions in the new earth, because there were lions in the old earth, and these lions will somehow be more majestic, more (in the good sense of the word) terrible than before without posing any of the danger that they did before. There will be tigers and bears too—oh my!—but we will coexist with them without fear. Isaiah paints a similar picture here:

The wolf shall dwell with the lamb,
  and the leopard shall lie down with the young goat,
and the calf and the lion and the fattened calf together;
  and a little child shall lead them. (11:6)

This is, presumably, what shalom among creatures looked like before the fall, and it is presumably what shalom restored will look like in the new earth. If God made something, you can believe he will remake it. And since death and danger are consequences of mankind's sin, once sin is vanquished and men are restored, all God's creatures will enjoy restored relationship with him, with man, and with each other.

We can expect, in fact, that all our animal friends will join us in the new heavens and new earth. Since grace is true, we can assume this includes snakes. And even cats, I guess.

Martin Luther saw the bigness of God's justifying of sinful mankind in the same way, assuming from the Bible's testimony about the new earth that if man is justified back into right relationship with God, what was cursed when that relationship was broken will then be restored. When his dog was suffering a particularly noisome barking fit, Martin supposedly preached this gospel implication to him, exhorting the pooch this way: "Never mind, little Hans . . . Thou too, in the Resurrection, shalt have a little golden tail."[4]

I'm looking at my own dog right now, even as I write this sentence. He is biting his butt. I hope this gets sorted out in the new earth. And I know if our dog could speak his own hopes for the world to come, he will want to not be afraid of thunder. We bought him something called a ThunderShirt, and it only serves to replace his fear with shame. I want to say to him, "Never mind, little Indi. In the resurrection, there will be no more Thunder Shirts." Maybe there will be no more thunder. But even if there is, I bet our neurotic

---

[4] Quoted in J. Hudson, "A Few More Words on Dogs," in *The Westminster Review*, vol. 150 (New York: Leonard Scott, 1898), 319.

little Indi will be prancing about in the middle of the rain, proud as a prince in the sunshine.

Maybe you think I'm taking this too far. Certainly there are people who love their pets too much. We can make idols of anything. And yet the affection we tend to have for our pets, and even the respect and awe and curiosity we tend to have for all other animals, seems to be rooted in the relationship God has himself set up between man and beast.

The animals were brought before Adam that he might name them. This connotes his dominion over them but also his relationship with them. Then we get to the second Adam and find him calling himself a shepherd. He says things like, "Which one of you who has a sheep, if it falls into a pit on the Sabbath, will not take hold of it and lift it out?" (Matt. 12:11) and, "Are not five sparrows sold for two pennies? And not one of them is forgotten before God" (Luke 12:6).

Everything was created to give God glory. When his glory finally crashes into earth in Christ's return, setting everything back to rights, all of creation will be restored to better than the good it was declared to be in the beginning. In this way, the actual vision God casts for the future of creation is better than the vision many Christians have for heaven. We look forward to a new heavens and a new earth, where the shalom between God and man and beast characterizes the glory-drenched earth once again.

So do all dogs go to heaven?

Yes. There, I said it.

No, actually, I don't know. Animals are not made in God's image like men and women are. They are fallen by extension of man's disobedience, not by their own sin, so they are not spoken of in the Scriptures in terms of needing salvation. Jesus did not die for our pets in the same way he died for us. Animals do not have souls in the same sense humans do. So whether our specific pets will be present in the age to come, we cannot say with any certainty. But it does seem that we can say there will be animals in the age to come, because God is planning to restore creation, and that includes animals. If by one man's disobedience came the curse upon the animal kingdom, then by the sinless obedience of Christ comes the animal kingdom's blessing.

So to consider what God does with our pets is no little matter. If our pets are so important to us, why could we assume God has not embedded importance in every "little thing" under heaven? He's embedded importance in everything.

Creation and Caring

If everything is important, ripe with glory, it doesn't mean that everything we think is important is important in quite the way we think it is. We may in fact be underemphasizing some things and overemphasizing others. We underemphasize when we deny an importance God establishes about something. We overemphasize when we see an importance in something that departs from God's priority of his own glory. Perhaps nowhere is this dichotomy more evident than in the two primary ways we tend to think about creation itself.

In the Western world, mankind tends to think either too much of creation or too little. We see a lot of the thinking too much of creation in non-Christian subcultures, among both atheistic naturalists and pseudospiritual New Agers. There are many people for whom nature is itself their god. And of course there are too many professing Christians who neglect things like Bible study and corporate worship because they prefer to experience God in the great outdoors. I'm reminded, though, of some more wise words from C. S. Lewis:

> In a way I quite remember why some people are put off by Theology. I remember once when I had been giving a talk to the R.A.F., an old, hard-bitten officer got up and said, "I've no use for all that stuff. But, mind you, I'm a religious man too. I know there's a God. I've felt Him: out alone in the desert at night: the tremendous mystery. And that's just why I don't

believe all your neat little dogmas and formulas about Him. To anyone who's met the real thing they all seem so petty and pedantic and unreal!"

Now in a sense I quite agreed with that man. I think he had probably had a real experience of God in the desert. And when he turned from that experience to the Christian creeds, I think he really was turning from something real to something less real. In the same way, if a man has once looked at the Atlantic from the beach, and then goes away and looks at a map of the Atlantic, he also will be turning from something real to something less real: turning from real waves to a bit of coloured paper. But here comes the point. The map is admittedly only coloured paper, but there are two things you have to remember about it. In the first place, it is based on what hundreds and thousands of people have found out by sailing the real Atlantic. In that way it has behind it masses of experience just as real as the one you could have from the beach; only, while yours would be a single glimpse, the map fits all those different experiences together. In the second place, if you want to go anywhere, the map is absolutely necessary. As long as you are content with walks on the beach, your own glimpses are far more fun than looking at a map. But the map is going to be more use than walks on the beach if you want to get to America.

Now, Theology is like the map.[5]

On the one hand, some people look at creation as the be-all and end-all, and they will be incredibly surprised on that day when creation gets better and they have to miss out. But if you follow nature's trail to nature's Maker and worship him alone, everything else will get thrown in with it. You can have those walks on the beach. You might even be able to walk across the oceans from continent to continent. This comes from believing not what you see right now, but from believing what you hear in the words in that map called the Bible.

On the other hand, some people care too little for creation. "This world is not my home," they say, but they've mistaken the

---

[5] C. S. Lewis, *Mere Christianity* (New York: HarperCollins, 2001), 153–54.

sinful way of the world's systems and the spiritual darkness at work in creation with the created world itself. The created world is our home, and it will be our home. And just because God is going to change it, to fix it, doesn't mean it's our job to contribute to its degradation.

Therefore, there is a way to care about creation too much and there is a way to care about creation too little. With Christ's gospel at the center of our lives and his restoration of the broken world in view, then, we can engage in respectful, diligent creation care that gives God glory.

If he declared the world good, why would we mistreat it? It is fallen, yes, but so are our neighbors, and God has commanded us to love them. One way we might love our neighbors, in fact, is by working to care for the world we all live in. This, in a sense, "makes the world a better place" but, more importantly, it casts a vision for the day when God actually makes the world a better place. With appropriate creation care—respecting our environments, reducing wastefulness and pollution, treating the animal world humanely, etc.—we depict God's future plans for the earth.

Still, God has a plan for everything. Not just for mankind and creation, but for what we make of it all.

OSAGE CITY PUBLIC LIBRARY
515 MAIN
OSAGE CITY, KS 66523

4

The Game of Thrones

God's Plan for Nations

I once walked from Mexico to Canada in thirty minutes. Along the way I sampled baklava in Morocco and bought a teapot in Japan. It was a wonderful trip. When I was done, I walked all the way back.

I love Disney's EPCOT Center. It's the only place you can stop off in England for fish and chips while taking a direct route from China to Norway. This part of EPCOT is called the World Showcase, and in this showcase the Disney corporation has sought to cram in everything light and lively about international culture into one pleasing, commoditized experience.

In a way, you could say that the World Showcase is Disney's attempt at creating a new earth. There are no border disputes. There are no wars. There aren't even any language or currency barriers.

And it all works because it crams the best of every nation into a Play-Doh cliché factory and unites it all under the magic and harmony of the very American reign of the Disney brand.

I sometimes wonder what foreign visitors think when visiting the EPCOT stand-in for their native land. Would it be like an American in a foreign land going to an America-themed park where

Coca-Cola, Michael Jackson, and apple pie were lauded as our hallmark cultural achievements?

In any event, what EPCOT succeeds in doing is casting a vision for a world united by a common ethos, a common interest. It's all a dream, of course, something that our nations have never been able to achieve in life outside the fairy tale world of the Happiest Place on Earth. But it cartoonishly gets at what our patriotic hearts all wish for—enjoying unity while maintaining our diversity, living in a peaceful world where every nation and culture is free to pursue their own unique identity without fear of or infringement upon others. This was certainly God's original design for civilization. But like everything else, it went awry as soon as man started taking his identity into his own hands.

Kingdoms Come

Psalm 2:1 asks the profound question, "Why do the nations rage and the peoples plot in vain?" Well, they rage and plot because nations and peoples are made up of individuals and every individual is a sinner. They rage and plot in vain because no matter how shrewd the scheming of man, no matter how well-devised the political strategy or how powerful the army, we are not in control of our destiny.

In Genesis 10:10 we see the word *kingdom* used for the very first time. The fall of Genesis 3 has corrupted man's ambition but it has not curtailed it. Genesis 10, in fact, charts the growth of nations as a direct result of God's command "to be fruitful and multiply." The blessing of immortality is gone, but the mandate to take dominion is not.

But the mess we see all around us, in our local and national cultures and in the international communities—government corruption, coercion and oppression, wars and war crimes, discrimination and injustice, inequalities of all kinds, human trafficking (the list goes on and on)—is a direct result of the potent combination of unbridled ambition and total depravity. Thus, every human kingdom is in need of redemption. Every single one.

As we've already seen, the historical trajectory of today's great mess of kingdoms is found in the early pages of the Bible—specifically in the example found in Genesis 10. In the same passage we find the word *kingdom* used for the first time, we find this historical anecdote:

> Cush fathered Nimrod; he was the first on earth to be a mighty man. He was a mighty hunter before the LORD. Therefore it is said, "Like Nimrod a mighty hunter before the LORD." (10:8–9)

At first glance, this looks like a positive description. Who wouldn't want to be a "mighty man" and a "mighty hunter before the LORD"? I mean, the only drawback is that your name is Nimrod.

But that name is important too, because the Hebrew word *Nimrod* means "rebel." And the sense of "mighty man" here is the same as in Genesis 6:4, where we learn that the offspring of the Nephilim were "mighty men of renown," which is *not a good thing*. Even "mighty hunter before the LORD" is not a good thing, because the hunting involved here is not really the kind you might do in the woods when deer season comes around, but is more like being a warrior against people, and it's all carried out in front of God's face, as it were, in spite of God's warnings against wickedness and bloodthirstiness. In their classic commentary on this passage, Keil and Delitzsch write, "[W]e must add to the literal meaning the figurative signification of a 'hunter of men' (a trapper of men by stratagem and force . . .); *Nimrod* the hunter became a tyrant, a powerful hunter of men."[1]

So Nimrod the Rebel was a representative of a growing type of person in the spread of the kingdoms of Genesis: a tyrant. He was a bloodthirsty nation-builder who established dominion through oppression and exploitation.

And the first fruit of his efforts we see listed is in that verse 10:

[1] C. F. Keil and F. Delitzsch, *Biblical Commentary on the Old Testament*, vol. 1: *The Pentateuch* (Grand Rapids, MI: Eerdmans, 1951), 166.

"The beginning of his kingdom was Babel . . ." It's the original game of thrones.

What we see, even after God wiped the slate clean and started fresh with righteous Noah and his covenant children, is that people are sinners. And everything they touch tends to get tainted with sin.

Every experiment in nation-building leads to corruption because sinners are involved. It doesn't even matter what kind of government or nation you build. In the case of dictatorships, we have seen how power-hungry, murderous people ascend to high positions and oppress their people. With the communist experiment, the premise is that a powerful government can ensure total equality and fairness across all citizens. But history has proven that the government of a communist nation, supposed to be a benevolent all-giving source of equalization, instead becomes the chief source of oppression. And even in democratic nations or representative republics, the intentions are great and the system itself is pretty sound, but because people are not essentially "good" but essentially sinful—that's the Bible talking here—you're going to end up with unchecked sin, especially when the majority of a nation has lost its moral compass.

There is no perfect form of earthly governance or nation. This is the reality testified to over and over again in the Bible, and it's the reality proved true over and over again through modern history. Whenever you put sinners in charge, you're going to have sin.

Making a Name for Ourselves

So we draw lines. We stake out our territories. God has put us out of the garden, but we keep trying to remake it with our laws and treaties and declarations, with our flags and our constitutions. What are we trying to do, exactly?

From Nimrod the bloodthirsty hunter we turn to the next chapter in God's story to see the towering ambition of the first kingdom-builders.

Now the whole earth had one language and the same words. And as people migrated from the east, they found a plain in the land of Shinar and settled there. And they said to one another, "Come, let us make bricks, and burn them thoroughly." And they had brick for stone, and bitumen for mortar. Then they said, "Come, let us build ourselves a city and a tower with its top in the heavens, and let us make a name for ourselves, lest we be dispersed over the face of the whole earth." And the LORD came down to see the city and the tower, which the children of man had built. And the LORD said, "Behold, they are one people, and they have all one language, and this is only the beginning of what they will do. And nothing that they propose to do will now be impossible for them. Come, let us go down and there confuse their language, so that they may not understand one another's speech." So the LORD dispersed them from there over the face of all the earth, and they left off building the city. Therefore its name was called Babel, because there the LORD confused the language of all the earth. And from there the LORD dispersed them over the face of all the earth. (Gen. 11:1–9)

People made in God's image are extraordinary. We do extraordinary things, and what's amazing is that these extraordinary things begin with just dreams and observations.

Man stared at the moon for thousands of years until he figured out a way to get up there.

Man kept looking at skin, at plant leaves, at dirt, coming up with ways to look more closely and more closely until finally he could see at the cellular level and start coming up with ideas about how these things work, and how you might fix them if they stopped working.

And man one day saw that the sun hardened clay into stone, so that if people lived in a place without much stone, they could "make bricks, and burn them thoroughly."

God has given us an amazing resource with these brains, and by making us in his own image, he has embedded in us creativity and innovation and an inventive and entrepreneurial spirit. So human beings are extraordinary, powerful creatures.

The problem is: We know this.

See, the problem with the building of the tower of Babel isn't that people built a tower. It's their *motivation* in building it.

Genesis 11:4 really tells us all we need to know: "Then they said, 'Come, let us build ourselves a city and a tower with its top in the heavens, and let us make a name for ourselves, lest we be dispersed over the face of the whole earth.'"

The first kingdom-builders were motivated by two primary things: fear and pride.

Fear and pride tend to go hand in hand, even though we don't often think of them working together or being similar. Fear has a superficial humility to it, a timidity that seems the opposite of pride. But to shrink back in fear—especially in disobedience to God's command—is to value your life more than God's command, to treasure your own safety over God's will. And this is exactly what is taking place in Genesis 11.

What are they afraid of? "Being dispersed over the face of the whole earth" (11:4). But God has given mankind the mandate to do that very thing: to be dispersed.

"And God said to them, 'Be fruitful and multiply and *fill the earth* and subdue it'" (Gen. 1:28).

"And God blessed Noah and his sons and said to them, 'Be fruitful and multiply and fill the earth'" (Gen. 9:1).

The main reason God wants mankind to "fill the earth" is to achieve his endgame for the world—that the knowledge of his glory will cover the earth (Hab. 2:14). He wants worship of himself to be planted everywhere, he wants all inhabitable space filled with worshipers, and he wants the inhabitable spaces made habitable so that worship of him can go up from there. He is God. He is great and greatly to be praised.

But the people in the land of Shinar are a bunch of Nimrods. "Come, let us build ourselves a city and a tower with its top in the heavens," they say, not as a monument to the glory of God, not as a sanctuary in which to worship the Lord, not as a base of operations from which to send out pioneers to uninhabited places, but to what? "To make a name for ourselves, lest we be dispersed over the face of the whole earth."

They were afraid of doing what God had commanded them to do, so they decided to circle the wagons, hunker down, consolidate their power and their strength, and channel their efforts into increasing their own glory.

This is a huge cautionary tale for God's churches today, by the way. Don't you think there's a lesson to be learned here about disobedience to God's mission to "go into all the world, making disciples of all peoples," even if our disobedience is not about antagonistic rebellion, but *fear*?

Fear lies behind the excuses a church makes to disobey God's call to be on mission:

We can't spare the people.

We don't have the money.

Why can't someone else do it?

It's taken such hard work to grow; why undo all that work?

And then fear and pride go hand in hand. A church making fearful excuses for disobeying God's call to mission begins to think only about herself—how she might build up herself, how she might increase her own glory. Gradually, eventually, the entire enterprise becomes not a monument to God's glory but a religious exercise in self-preservation and self-congratulations.

I think we've got some modern examples of this.

Many of the empty church buildings dotting the New England rural landscape got that way because of the mistaken notion that centering on people's innate goodness and questioning God's Word is what leads to success. Historically and statistically, this leads to institutional demise. We've seen it over and over again. The monuments to human potential are now memorials to empty religion.

Perhaps the most vivid examples of religion in pursuit of the building of a personal kingdom, "making a name for one's self," that we have seen in our own day are the aspirations of televangelists. The most Tower of Babel-esque monument to religiously missing the point might be the Crystal Cathedral in Garden Grove, Orange County, California. Have you seen this thing? It's like something out of *Logan's Run* or even EPCOT. According to Wikipedia:

> The reflective glass building, designed by American architect Philip Johnson, was completed in 1981 and seats 2,736 people. The largest glass building in the world, it has one of the largest musical instruments in the world, the Hazel Wright Memorial organ.

Inside the Crystal Cathedral, for nearly thirty years, Robert Schuller preached under the auspices of the Reformed Church in America a sort of moralistic therapeutic deism masquerading as biblical Christianity, a message beamed into millions of homes via the Crystal Cathedral's television program *The Hour of Power*. Schuller became a very wealthy televangelist due to the Crystal Cathedral's success and his own publishing efforts. One of his books is titled *If You Can Dream It, You Can Do It.* (And no, there isn't a picture of the Tower of Babel on the cover.)

In his book *Self-Esteem: The New Reformation*, Schuller mixes up belief in Christ with belief in one's self, writing:

> And I can feel the self-esteem rising all around me and within me, "Rivers of living water shall flow from the inmost being of anyone who believes in me" (John 7:38). I'll really feel good about myself.[2]

Later in the same book, he writes:

> What is the basic flaw? I believe is it the failure to proclaim the gospel in a way that can satisfy every person's deepest need— one's spiritual hunger for glory. Rather than glorify God's highest creation—the human being—Christian liturgies, hymns,

---

[2] Robert H. Schuller, *Self-Esteem: The New Reformation* (Waco, Texas: Word, 1982), 80.

prayers, and scriptural interpretations have often insensitively and destructively offended the dignity of the person.[3]

Indeed, Schuller's entire message is predicated on avoiding the topic of sin, so as not to offend anybody, and working at, as he says, glorifying the human being.

This message sells really well. We want to be glorified. Because of original sin, we all in our flesh want to believe the lie hissed to Adam and Eve: "You can be like God."

Robert Schuller once said that no church has a money problem; it only has an idea problem. In 2010, the Crystal Cathedral declared bankruptcy. His children got locked into a great conflict after his passing, arguing over money and the rights to his publishing and broadcasting empire. They've sold the Crystal Cathedral to the local Catholic Diocese, and it will be reopened soon as a place of Roman Catholic worship. The monument built on positive thinking and "if you can believe it, you can achieve it" gobbledygook has crumbled.

Do you see what happens when we build a tower to ourselves, to the glorification of human beings rather than to God?

This is not to say that if a church or a Christian stays faithful, they will always see growth and success. We have enough biblical and historical examples to know there are no guarantees. But every monument we build to make a name for ourselves will be crushed eventually. Every one of our Babel towers has an expiration date engraved in it by the Lord God.

We have to understand that great falls are not just what happens to "those people." They can happen to "us people" too, and we evangelicals in the United States of America must remember this as we seek to co-opt the biblical message to the people of Israel and to the cross-cultural church as pertaining to our national aspirations. The hope of the world is not America, but Jesus. And mixing up the two has been a subtle building of Babel towers for too many Christians.

This is why even churches that engage in mission, that determine

---

[3] Ibid., 31.

to send out and spread out and plant worship in other places and send believers to the corners of the earth, can still set themselves up for failure if they are doing it all for their own glory.

Perhaps when Solomon wrote Proverbs 16:18, he had a mental image of the Tower of Babel: "Pride goes before destruction, and a haughty spirit before a fall." Because this is what happens next:

> And the LORD came down to see the city and the tower, which the children of man had built. And the LORD said, "Behold, they are one people, and they have all one language, and this is only the beginning of what they will do. And nothing that they propose to do will now be impossible for them. Come, let us go down and there confuse their language, so that they may not understand one another's speech." So the LORD dispersed them from there over the face of all the earth, and they left off building the city. (Gen. 11:5–8)

First of all, the language of verse 5 is very intentional: "The LORD came down to see the city." They built a tower to the heavens! As tall as they could get it! And God was like, "What's that speck down there? Let me check that out. Ohh, nice tower you've got here. Oh yes, very tall. I almost knocked it over with my pinky toe."

The way Moses narrates this development—"the LORD came down to see the city and the tower"—is very sarcastic. And it sets up the truth of God's glory in comparison to our own.

Verse 6 can be a little confusing, because it sounds like man's potential is limitless and God is worried about that. But the feeling is similar to Genesis 3:22–23:

> Then the LORD God said, "Behold, the man has become like one of us in knowing good and evil. Now, lest he reach out his hand and take also of the tree of life and eat, and live forever—" therefore the LORD God sent him out from the garden of Eden to work the ground from which he was taken.

We can see how mankind keeps playing out the history of the fall.

We take a good gift and turn it into idolatry and God punishes idolatry, but there's always a mercy embedded in it. In Genesis 11:6, God is not worried about our potential; he is protecting us from ourselves. In other words, he is saying, "If we"—speaking to his Trinitarian self—"let them go on this way, the extent of their idolatry will be limitless!" Thus, in verse 7, God messes them up.

There is no other way to take this passage. It is a direct, divine intervention, and we have no biblical or spiritual reason not to take it at face value and interpret it as a historical event. God in great power, by his Spirit, rewired their brains to contain different patterns of speech and then kicked them all out. They couldn't talk to each other anymore and they couldn't understand each other anymore, so they lost their unity. The dispersion likely was a part of this confusion of speech; the dispersion of languages fractured them all into tinier tribes and peoples, and so they ended up going off with the few they could each understand and spreading out.

God will have his way, one way or another. So you can get there the willing way or the hard way. But there's no getting around what he wants. (Just ask Jonah.)

So the kingdom-builders are now left with linguistic disunity and geographic dispersion. The people had a unity and a collective strength, but it was all in service to themselves. And this always leads to destruction.

There is a good kind of patriotism, to be sure. God has mandated nation-building, but for his own glory, not the glory of the nations. When we build kingdoms predicated on human potential, human achievement, and human exaltation, we will always fall far short of heaven. You can even pattern national laws after God's law—and you should!—but if it's all an exercise in self-righteousness, it will not ultimately last. Pharisaical kingdoms fall just like worldly kingdoms.

Wretched people that we are, who will rescue us from these monuments of death? How will we get from the chaos of self-interest and the disunity of our rebellion against God's glory to the right kind of power, the right kind of unity? How can our kingdoms reach the right kind of connection and significance?

Well, remember that secret to the universe, the gospel.

When we believe the good news—that Jesus Christ died to forgive the great fundamental sin of idolatry and rose again in a glorified body to give us the kind of glory we really need, eternal life in and with him—it is all because the Lord God has come down to our ruined cities. He has come down from heaven in Jesus Christ to survey the wreckage up close, to look into our messy hearts, to examine the conflict and the chaos and the fear and the pride and the dishonorable disobedience, and he crushes the towers of Babel we have built up in our hearts.

We may fear we cannot be loved, we may fear we cannot be forgiven, we may fear we're the heart way too hard for God to do anything with, but he laughs. "Oh, you think *you're* the nut I can't crack? I've finally met my match? No, nothing I propose to do is impossible for me."

And his Spirit sets up shop. In a great historical rematch, we see in the outbreak of the gospel the dam of God's glory broken open to pour out floods of living water on all peoples. In the very story God is telling in history, we see the great reversal and redemption of Babel.

Babel Restored

When Jesus and his disciples come in ministry, they come saying, "Repent, for the kingdom of heaven is at hand!" (Matt. 4:17).

The kingdom is God's rule; it is the manifest presence of God's sovereignty. It is this kingdom that we ought to be focused on, above all others. One throne rules them all, and it is Christ's.

In Daniel 2, King Nebuchadnezzar has a bizarre dream that troubles him deeply. He feels it is a signal from the spiritual plane of existence and he wants to know the meaning. He asks his trusted magicians and sorcerers to interpret it, but he tests their connection to the secret world by first asking them to reveal his dream. In other words, he doesn't want to just tell them what he dreamed and have them make up some kind of significance for it. He wants to know they really see into the other world by having them retell his dream to him. Of course none of them can do it.

But Daniel walks with God. Daniel is a prophet. Daniel receives the signals from the Spirit's deep space. Daniel reveals Nebuchadnezzar's dream and interprets it. He informs the king about the rise and fall of future kingdoms. How can he know this? Because God knows it. God is telling the story of these kingdoms, ultimately. We try to write our own glory across the heavens, and God laughs.

In the end, Daniel tells the king that he sees a mighty kingdom forged from the rock that smashes all earthly kingdoms because it is not of this world. He's talking about the kingdom of God.

It is the reality of the kingdom of God—and the gospel purpose in it to glorify Christ—that should comfort Christians today, not the rising and falling of popular opinion or the ways of the Supreme Court or the majority votes in the Congress or the moral sanity of the president. All those people are sinners. We can root for them and persuade them and pray for them and hope for them—but we cannot hope *in* them, because none of them is not a sinner. Only Jesus Christ's kingdom comes with perfect grace and peace and justice. And only Jesus Christ's kingdom will remain.

But what's wonderful about Jesus Christ's kingdom is that even though he is smashing all the corrupt systems and sinful governments and tyrannies and injustice, he is also *redeeming* the nations oppressed by sin, planning to restore them through his perfect kingship.

So he comes first to the nation of Israel but not only to them: "I have other sheep that are not of this fold," he says (John 10:16). And he reaches out to the Gentiles—to the Canaanites, to the Samaritans, to the Ethiopians, and to the Egyptians, to all the sons of Shem, yes, but to all the sons of Ham and Japheth too.

And so when Genesis 10:32 charts the beginning of mankind's broken kingdom-building, saying, "from these the nations spread abroad on the earth after the flood," it is also charting the length of Christ's reach.

This is the reach of Christ's kingdom on earth. Wherever there is a nation, Christ is King. As Abraham Kuyper has famously said, "There is not a square inch in the whole domain of our human existence over which Christ, who is Sovereign over *all*, does not cry: 'Mine!'"[4]

And Christ's kingship must be proclaimed, because we are told that the end will not come until all the nations have heard (Matt. 24:14). So Jesus tells his disciples, "Go therefore and make disciples of *all nations*, baptizing them in the name of the Father and of the Son and of the Holy Spirit" (Matt. 28:19). We should probably not interpret "nations" in these verses to correspond neatly to every bordered country in the world, but rather to every people group in the world. Revelation 7:9 expands "every nation" to refer to "all tribes and peoples and languages."

Thus, Genesis 10 is not just a genealogy or a table of nations. It is a catalog of all that Christ rules and all that Christ will redeem. No, not every single individual will be redeemed, but individuals from every tongue, tribe, race, and nation will trust in him for forgiveness of sins and the gift of eternal life.

Behold he is making all things new. Even the sinful kingdoms of the world. We see this in the way God's story doubles back on itself to revisit his Babel judgment. Even the toppled tower will be restored for God's glory.

Luke tells the story this way:

> When the day of Pentecost arrived, they were all together in one place. And suddenly there came from heaven a sound like a mighty rushing wind, and it filled the entire house where they were sitting. And divided tongues as of fire appeared to them and rested on each one of them. And they were all filled with

---

[4] Abraham Kuyper, inaugural lecture at the Free University of Amsterdam, October 20, 1880, quoted in *Abraham Kuyper: A Centennial Reader*, ed. James D. Bratt (Grand Rapids, MI: Eerdmans, 1998), 488.

the Holy Spirit and began to speak in other tongues as the Spirit gave them utterance.

Now there were dwelling in Jerusalem Jews, devout men from every nation under heaven. And at this sound the multitude came together, and they were bewildered, because each one was hearing them speak in his own language. And they were amazed and astonished, saying, "Are not all these who are speaking Galileans? And how is it that we hear, each of us in his own native language? Parthians and Medes and Elamites and residents of Mesopotamia, Judea and Cappadocia, Pontus and Asia, Phrygia and Pamphylia, Egypt and the parts of Libya belonging to Cyrene, and visitors from Rome, both Jews and proselytes, Cretans and Arabians—we hear them telling in our own tongues the mighty works of God." And all were amazed and perplexed, saying to one another, "What does this mean?" (Acts 2:1–12)

What God has torn apart, let no man try to join together. Only the Spirit can straighten what he has bent. Only the Spirit can order what he has disordered. To stifle Babel's attempts at self-worship, God confused their language and spread them out. Now to galvanize their hearts in worship to him alone, God unites them through their languages and gathers them up.

What God has done by his Spirit at Pentecost is make good on his promise to bare his glory "before the eyes of all the nations," that "all the ends of the earth shall see the salvation of our God" (Isa. 52:10). "The nations shall see your righteousness," Isaiah 62:2 says. God is fulfilling his own nation-building covenant, "seeing that Abraham shall surely become a great and mighty nation, and all the nations of the earth shall be blessed in him" (Gen. 18:18).

And at Pentecost we have a glimpse into the great redemption to come. When God's kingdom in Christ is finally consummated at the end of days, and that new city comes down from heaven to take splendid dominion on earth, "by its light will the nations walk, and the kings of the earth will bring their glory into it" (Rev. 21:24).

The kings of nations will bring their glory into the throne room of God to give it to him. Because he alone deserves it. Because he is God, and because, by the power of his Spirit, the gospel of Jesus Christ is true.

This is hope for the future that makes election results look like a trifle.

Finding our true identity—our fulfilling connection and significance—in Christ and his church makes all of our previous kingdom-building, throne-sitting, flag-waving cultural and imperial ambitions seem like a black hole of nothingness. Before, we weren't even a people. But now? We are the new humanity, redeemed in Christ.

The New Humanity's Posture

So now we've seen that as ambitious and as big as man's first kingdom-builders got, they could not outrun the dominion God had over *them*. No nations or kingdoms are a surprise to him. They are each part of his sovereign plan, which is why Genesis 10 exists in the first place—to show how all that man is doing fits into the big story of creation and fall and redemption that God is telling through history.

In fact, we learn throughout the Bible that God rules over all. He is sovereign over all. And this includes the machinations of every kingdom on earth. Consider these truths:

"For kingship belongs to the LORD, and he rules over the nations" (Ps. 22:28).

"The king's heart is a stream of water in the hand of the LORD; he turns it wherever he will" (Prov. 21:1).

God says through Moses to Pharaoh, "But for this purpose I have raised you up, to show you my power, so that my name may be proclaimed in all the earth" (Ex. 9:16).

God's purpose will be fulfilled. You cannot thwart his plan!

This is good news, especially as it relates to the gospel, because if God were not sovereign over all that takes place here in the nations on earth, we should be in full-on despair mode. And if our hope is in us, in the church, in politics, in our abilities to finally "get it right," we should despair, because we keep messing it up. Only knowing that God is in control and that his purposes will stand should get us up in the morning feeling hopeful.

In the Western world we have been tracking a cultural downgrade for some time. To simply say what the Bible says—as one who believes what it says, of course, not as some gawker agog at its impoliteness—is sometimes considered defamatory, thought crime, or hate speech. It is offensive. "There oughta be a law against this!" the sensitive sinner cries.

In response to such outrage, Christians must first be soberminded. We do not face martyrdom—at least, not yet.

But we have to also be honest. The trend is downward. Preaching the politically incorrect truths of the Bible is an actual crime in some "civilized" nations, and we would be arrogant to act like such laws could never be enacted here. Already believers are facing fines and in some cases imprisonment for binding their conscience to God's laws, particularly as it relates to sexual immorality.

Let's remember that every unfree nation got unfree while making great assurances to its people.

But let's be hopeful in the gospel. God is sovereign. Let's remember exactly who's in charge here. The Western world may be trending downward, but the situation is never so grim as all that. We may get what we don't deserve but we will be getting exactly what we've been promised. "In this world you will have trouble . . ." (John 16:33 NIV). "Do not be surprised, brothers, that the world hates you" (1 John 3:13). Our sovereign Lord isn't making this all up as he goes along. The Trinity holds no emergency sessions.

"Take heart," Jesus continues in John 16:33. "I have overcome the world."

Christ the Lord sustains the universe by his powerful word, he declares the end from the beginning, he laughs kings to scorn (Ps. 2:4), he walks on the stormy waters, he stirs the mighty seas, he makes the mountains his footstool, he brims with sovereign glory from everlasting to everlasting. He is God.

And so:

Will we bear the derision and disgrace? Yes, and we will count it wealth (Heb. 11:26).

Will we suffer the plundering of our property? Yes, and we will count it joy (Heb. 10:34).

Will we suffer division in our families and communities? Yes, and we will count it worthiness of Christ (Matt. 10:37).

Let us be resolute together, as the new humanity of God, to agree that whatever makes us more like Jesus, be it comfort or cross, is authorized by God, and let us believe he will not take anything needful away from us that he won't return to us a millionfold. Let us have the posture bowed to God's sovereignty, boasting in Christ's greatness, much more so than we bow to fear or pride, much more so than we clamor about our own rights and honors.

What makes us a citizen of heaven is much better than what makes us a citizen of our respective nations, as great a privilege as that is. And because we are citizens of heaven, this means that no matter how bad and bloodthirsty the kingdoms of this world get, the situation cannot ever for us get desperate. The Christian is united with Christ, seated with him (Eph. 2:6), hidden with him in God (Col. 3:3), indivisible from him by life or death (John 10:29; Rom. 8:38–39). Therefore, the Christian is as secure as Christ himself. He has escaped the prideful game of thrones and been ushered right into the heavenly throne room of grace.

With his eyes set on the kingdom of God held by God's sovereign purposes, Martin Luther declared: "World, death, devil, hell, away and leave me in peace! You have no hold on me. If you will not let me live, then I will die. But you won't succeed in that. Chop my head off, and it won't harm me. I have One who will give me a new one."[5]

Let's not let our hearts be tuned to the newspaper headlines.

---

[5] *Off the Record with Martin Luther: An Original Translation of the Table Talks*, trans. Charles Daudert (Kalamazoo, MI: Hansa-Hewlett, 2009), 402.

Let's not let our hearts be tuned to the rising and falling of earthly kingdoms. God is on the throne.

And one of the ways God shows in the Bible his sovereignty over the rise and fall of kingdoms throughout history is by preserving the nation of Israel in and out of countless dangers, through captivity and enslavement, through wars and oppressions, through dispersions and corruptions. He sides with them not because they are strong or even because they are righteous but because they are *his*. This is the church's truth too. The new humanity is not divided by borders and flags; it is united across them by God's kingdom, which is in our very midst (Luke 17:21).

The New Humanity's Politics

St. Augustine's classic *The City of God* (426 AD) is a great piece of theology and philosophy. Ever since the Visigoths sacked Rome in 410 AD, the Romans had been questioning how their empire had become so weak. They decided to blame the Christians. Since by that time Christianity and the Roman Empire had become fairly intertwined, many Romans believed that by gradually abandoning their Roman religion—worship of gods and of the emperors—for cultural Christianity, they had made themselves vulnerable.

So Augustine wrote *The City of God* both to rebut the idea that Christianity makes a nation weak and to console Christians who might be confused as well, and who were under attack from their countrymen. The primary way Augustine did this was by contrasting the earthly kingdom with the heavenly kingdom, what he called the City of Man versus the City of God. He wrote, for instance, that "Incomparably more glorious than Rome, is that heavenly city in which for victory you have truth; for dignity, holiness; for peace, felicity; for life, eternity."[6]

When we grasp this important contrast, our hearts will direct our politics differently. For one thing, our hearts will not be tuned

---

[6] Augustine, *The City of God*, trans. Marcus Dods (New York: Random House, 1950), 2.73.

to politics! But for another, we will employ our earthly politics in the service of heaven's agenda.

Deep down, it is the heavenly city we really long for. And through the rise and fall of all these nations chronicled throughout the Bible, it is the heavenly city that remains and comes crashing through space and time into first-century Palestine when the four Gospels begin. And it is the heavenly city that will endure beyond all time.

> Of the increase of his government and of peace
> there will be no end,
> on the throne of David and over his kingdom,
> to establish it and to uphold it
> with justice and with righteousness
> from this time forth and forevermore. (Isa. 9:7)

American Christians must remember this. It keeps us from becoming politically stupid and idolatrous. Pastor and author Eugene Peterson writes:

> I believe that the kingdoms of this world, American and Venezuelan and Chinese, will become the kingdom of our God and Christ, and I believe the new kingdom is already among us. That is why I'm a pastor, to introduce people to the real world and train them to live in it. I learned early that the methods of my work must correspond to the realities of the kingdom. The methods that make the kingdom of America strong—economic, military, technological, informational—are not suited to making the kingdom of God strong. I have had to learn a new methodology: truth-telling and love-making, prayer and parable. These are not methods very well adapted to raising the standard of living in suburbia or massaging the ego into a fashionable shape.
>
> But America and suburbia and the ego compose my parish. Most of the individuals in this amalgam suppose that the goals they have for themselves and the goals God has for them are the same. It is the oldest religious mistake: refusing to countenance any real difference between God and us, imagining God to be a

vague extrapolation of our desires, and then hiring a priest to manage the affairs between self and the extrapolation. And I, one of the priests they hired, am having none of it.

But if I'm not willing to help them become what they want to be, what am I doing taking their pay? I am being subversive. I am undermining the kingdom of self and establishing the kingdom of God. I am helping them to become what God wants them to be, using the methods of subversion.[7]

Peterson is right to direct Christians toward subversion. That is true kingdom work—or, rather, it is the work of the true kingdom. It does not seek obliteration of all towers, only the redeeming of them.

The mandate for believers in Christ is to now "tell the story"—to tell the story of the true kingdom of God, how that kingdom answers the heart's cry of every worldly attempt at kingdom-building. In some sense, what we are meant to do is proclaim and embody the reality of God's kingdom and the world that is coming upon Christ's return within the midst of all the earth's pretenders to the throne.

America is beautiful, as is every land on God's green earth. And it is great to enjoy the blessings and privileges of our nation. But one day we shall see America as she really is, the truer and better America that is breaking through this glorious, groaning America, when the knowledge of God's glory covers it from sea to shining sea. This will not be upon any presidential election or upon the adding of any particular law, however, but upon Christ's return. Some of us are very glad to live in America. Even so, come quickly, Lord Jesus.

Because the church is a people "set apart," it now relates to the world and its institutions differently. Christians have a belief beyond borders and transcending politics. Because the church is united to Christ in heaven, she is never really at ease with the sociopolitical machinations of the world (or, at least, she shouldn't be).

---

[7] Eugene Peterson, *The Contemplative Pastor: Returning to the Art of Spiritual Direction* (Grand Rapids, MI: Eerdmans, 1989), 28.

But we often find the church falling victim to the false dichotomies of the world. Some Christians put too much hope in the political arena. Some Christians put none.

But are these our only options? Political idolatry on the one hand and political silence on the other? Shall we presume to protect the gospel's relevance by cordoning it off from certain areas of our life? The church all over the world—not just in the West—has real problems figuring out how to press the gospel into every corner of the cultural room, as it were, without it getting walked all over.

So what should the new humanity of the church's politics look like? What does real kingdom subversion do in the world of corrupt, rival kingdom-building?

I do think the Word of God helps us navigate these things. The apostle Peter describes the new "politics" of the new humanity like this:

> Beloved, I urge you as sojourners and exiles to abstain from the passions of the flesh, which wage war against your soul. Keep your conduct among the Gentiles honorable, so that when they speak against you as evildoers, they may see your good deeds and glorify God on the day of visitation.
>
> Be subject for the Lord's sake to every human institution, whether it be to the emperor as supreme, or to governors as sent by him to punish those who do evil and to praise those who do good. For this is the will of God, that by doing good you should put to silence the ignorance of foolish people. Live as people who are free, not using your freedom as a cover-up for evil, but living as servants of God. Honor everyone. Love the brotherhood. Fear God. Honor the emperor. (1 Pet. 2:11–17)

So, in light of the story God is telling with the world, how does the church play the game of thrones?

Well, first, Peter reminds the brethren that their citizenship is in heaven ("sojourners and exiles"). This world is not our home, so we should not live like our ultimate treasure is anything temporary, whether it be good or bad or neutral. As it pertains to the Christian and politics, "abstain from the passions of the flesh" is really important. We are used to thinking of drunkenness and sexual immorality and the like in relation to that phrase, but it is equally applicable to political zealotry. Too many of us indulge the passions of the flesh when it comes to treating our candidates like messiahs and the other candidates like devils, and assuming laws and leaders and our land itself is the hope of the world. All of this is passing away, and we ought to treat it like it is.

And yet Peter is not necessarily advocating a withdrawal from the system. He is advocating honorable citizenship, a participation that commends the gospel of the kingdom. The level of political participation will vary from Christian to Christian, culture to culture, as conscience and conviction demands. Certainly there is no biblical legality for voting or not voting, politicking or not politicking. Let us be ruled by the Spirit in the matters on which the Scriptures are silent. But whether we vote or don't vote, campaign or don't campaign, let us do all things to the glory of God. This means at the very least, living upright, honorable, charitable, respectful lives as witness to our real citizenship. It also means not buying into the political idolatry of any side, playing tit for tat, spinning the truth, or lying or embracing hypocrisy or whitewashing our problematic candidates. It means refraining from rhetoric that reveals we worship false gods. Let's be respectable and respectful participants.

Second, Peter encourages the brethren to be subject to the human governmental and civic institutions "for the Lord's sake." (See also Paul's words in Rom. 13:1–7.) We obey the laws that do not violate God's laws, and we do so with the commendation of Christ in mind. So when we have to pay our taxes, we pay our taxes with Christ in mind. And if we vote, we vote with Christ in mind. We vote, but as John Piper says, we "vote as if not voting":

> Christians should deal with the world. This world is here to be used. Dealt with. There is no avoiding it. Not to deal with it is to deal with it *that* way. Not to weed your garden is to cultivate a weedy garden. Not to wear a coat in Minnesota is to freeze—to

deal with the cold that way. Not to stop when the light is red is to spend your money on fines or hospital bills and deal with the world that way. We must deal with the world.

But as we deal with it, we don't give it our fullest attention. We don't ascribe to the world the greatest status. There are unseen things that are vastly more precious than the world. We use the world without offering it our whole soul. We may work with all our might when dealing with the world, but the full passions of our heart will be attached to something higher—Godward purposes. We use the world, but not as an end in itself. It is a means. We deal with the world in order to make much of Christ.

So it is with voting. We deal with the system. We deal with the news. We deal with the candidates. We deal with the issues. But we deal with it all as if not dealing with it. It does not have our fullest attention. It is not the great thing in our lives. Christ is. And Christ will be ruling over his people with perfect supremacy no matter who is elected and no matter what government stands or falls. So we vote as though not voting.[8]

"Live as people who are free," Peter says. We will not be tied to any particular political or legislative outcomes as if our ultimate hope or devastation is tied to them. We will not let our affections be owned by who is in the statehouse or the White House.

"Live as servants of God," Peter says, and here we get another perspective on what it means to live as people who are free in a politicized world. It means participating respectfully and respectably, but it also means living as those whose ultimate allegiance is to God and not men. In Acts 5:27–29, when the apostles are brought before the authorities to be reminded of the law restricting their freedom to preach the gospel, the answer the apostles provide is not mute submission. They say, "We must obey God rather than men." We are beholden ultimately to God, not our political party or the American government, so when we are called to violate God's commands, we cannot obey. Indeed, when we see systemic sins and injustices

---

[8] John Piper, "Let Christians Vote as Though They Were Not Voting," *Desiring God* (blog), October 22, 2008, http://www.desiringgod.org/articles/let-christians-vote-as-though-they-were-not-voting/.

promoted and protected by the powers that be, as servants of God we are required to be bold prophets.

The Bible provides quite a history of the unique role of God's community speaking truth to power. Think Moses to Pharaoh, Nathan to David, Daniel and friends to Nebuchadnezzar, the prophets to the kings, John the Baptist to Herod, and the apostles to everybody in saying "Jesus is Lord" in the day of the Caesars. No, they did not conflate the kingdom of God with the kingdom of the world, and no, they did not conflate gospel with legislation, but they were not silent about the kingdom's opposition to injustice and immorality. And churchmen of conscience have maintained this same responsibility time and time again throughout history, acting and speaking directly to say the gospel's "No" to the political world's gross injustices.

The reforms throughout history pertaining to slavery, civil rights, orphans, care for the poor, AIDS in Africa, and now abortion and sex trafficking were and are the result of seeing these problems as gospel issues requiring the moral compass of the church to speak boldly and prophetically. We can most certainly deny that everything is the gospel while maintaining that the gospel helps us know how to think and talk about everything.

Peter closes this way: "Honor everyone. Love the brotherhood. Fear God. Honor the emperor." Notice the parallels between "everyone" and "the emperor." They are due honor. The church is distinguished as being owed love, not because all others do not deserve love but because the household of faith, as the family that endures eternally, receives a special loving allegiance above the world and its rulers. The gates of hell will prevail against the gates of cultures and kingdoms. But not the church. And Peter roots it all—familial love for the brethren and the honor kind of love for everybody else—in "fear of God." Where is our reverence due? Where is our worship due? Where are our affections due? They are due the gracious God who loves us, saves us, redeems us, secures us, and promises us the glory to come.

Therefore we will be faithful proclaimers of this God and his kingdom through stubborn fixation on his gospel. The gospel is our plumb line for discerning between activism and apathy in all things.

We resolve to be honorable citizens in this world because we are citizens of another, and we resolve to boldly speak truth to power because we must obey God rather than men, and we resolve to know nothing except Christ and him crucified, because he is the hope of the politically idolatrous world.

The importance of the church—and the fundamental purpose of the church—is to keep pointing away from the world for the hope of the world. While everyone else points to government, family, good deeds, and whatever else as The Secret, the church keeps pointing to the alien, heavenly power of grace as the hope for our problems and for *our false hopes*.

The gospel is the solution not just for behavioral sins of disobedience but for spiritual sins of idolatry, like looking to government, family, good deeds, and whatever else for salvation. Only the gospel is the answer to everything. And only the gospel makes us new and satisfies our longings for connection (with God and with our fellow man) and for significance in the world.

5

Non-Trivial Pursuit

God's Plan for Art, Science, and Work

Ever played Trivial Pursuit? There are umpteen versions available now, but I remember when the original, now-classic Trivial Pursuit board game—called the "Genus Edition"—was first released. I was just a kid, but I loved playing with my adult relatives and showing off how much knowledge I really had. It didn't bother me that all this knowledge was declared by the name of the game itself "trivial." Competing against grown-ups in questions of geography, history, and the like made me feel pretty non-trivial.

If you're not familiar with the game, the purpose is to travel around the board collecting triangular pie pieces to complete your game piece. There are six pieces in all, and once you correctly answer questions in each six categories on their designated pie piece space, you can make your way to the center of the board, where you then have to answer a question from a category of your opponents' choosing.

The first pieces of the pie I'd shoot for were pink and brown:

Entertainment and Arts & Literature. Those were my jam. I could answer questions on movies several decades before my time just as well as my elders, and nobody could match me in questions of A. A. Milne, Geoffrey Chaucer, or Pablo Picasso. (I liked the idea of the Sports & Leisure category too, but there were way too many questions about card games and horse racing for me to feel confident.)

Usually I would quickly collect pink and brown pie pieces and then spend the rest of the game putting off the green: Science & Nature. Yuck. I did not care for science at all. And if by chance I was able to finally land that green pie piece and make it to the center of the board, guess which category my loving relatives would throw at me to ensure I sat there forever?

What I liked about Trivial Pursuit was feeling smart. But it was more than that, actually. It was about feeling cultured. It's the same reason every couch potato loves *Jeopardy*. You can, for a moment at least, feel like a genius. (Or a "genus," whatever that is.)

But Trivial Pursuit is a lot like EPCOT's World Showcase. It takes every category of thing into its view and smooshes it down into something packaged and programmed in order to give its players a false sense of something real. At EPCOT, it's a projection of our longing for a new earth where every nation is the best of itself and coexists harmoniously with others. In Trivial Pursuit, it's a projection of our longing to be well-cultured, well-read, brilliant even. It's the projection of our desire *to know*.

So each aspect of culture gets a little slice of the pie. And we get to feel for a day like we rule the world, or at least the dining room. What we do in Trivial Pursuit, though, is what we are trying to do in the world at large—feel connected, feel significant. To be masters of something. This is not a trivial pursuit. But in the world after the fall of man, it can actually be quite a dangerous one.

The Beginning of Culture

What are we talking about when we talk about *culture*? Lots of people have tried to define the word, but what all the definitions typically boil down to is the collective aspirations of a given people in a particular time as expressed through what they produce (or "cultivate"). This includes things created like arts and entertainment, of course, but also things discovered or hypothesized in science or ambitions pursued and achievements accrued in various vocations. What we call culture is the reflection of whatever it is a given people are trying to cultivate.

And what we try to cultivate is largely driven by our values and desires, which is why when people define "culture," they often speak of a people group's belief systems or traditions. In short, we tend to cultivate what we worship. And we also tend to worship what we cultivate. That's the bizarre catch-22 of people and culture. Sometimes we hear Christian critics talk about the church being influenced by "the culture." But the culture is not some force or entity out in the ether, influencing people unilaterally. The culture is influenced by people; the culture *is* people.

So then, when Christian critics talk about influencing the culture, what we ought to hear is "influencing people." We ought to understand that when a Christian goes to the movie theater and buys a ticket to a particular show, or when he tunes his TV to a particular program, and even when he goes to work and puts in eight to ten hours in his office or on the assembly line at the factory, he is influencing the culture just as much as when he's writing those movies or designing whatever's being produced in the factory.

The problem is not so much with "culture" per se. It is with people and the kind of worship with which they drive their cultural influence.

Let's go way back to the early days of God's story to see how this all began. Genesis 4 shows us the roots of culture. In this chapter we are fresh off the fall of mankind (in Genesis 3), and we encounter the first murder in history. Adam's firstborn son Cain has killed his brother Abel. Why? Out of envy, mostly, because God accepted Abel's offering and not Cain's.

In a severe mercy similar to covering Adam and Eve with animal skins, God marks Cain (4:15). And like the curse upon Adam and Eve, God curses the ground on account of Cain and sends him into exile as a fugitive. What is the very next thing we see Cain do? He builds a city (4:17).

On the surface there is some good here. In a way, Genesis 4:17–22 reflects exactly the mandate God had given to Adam and Eve: be fruitful and multiply, fill the earth and subdue it, take dominion. In other words: build civilization, create culture.

But we see the departure from God's plan right away in 4:19. A man named Lamech took two wives. This was not how God designed marriage to work in the culture he wants us to create. It's not what he intended family to look like. It's a departure from his will. Lamech is trying to write his own story about marriage and family and thus culture.

So even as we see in this chapter some order develop toward civilization, we also see how self-centered civilization became right from the start.

Then, in Genesis 4:20–22, note the developments of agriculture, arts, and industry:

> Jabal . . . was the father of those who dwell in tents and have livestock. Jubal . . . was the father of all those who play the lyre and pipe . . . Tubal-cain . . . was the forger of all instruments of bronze and iron.

These people are creating culture, everything that makes a society worth living in. And this is coming from Cain. He has "built a city."

But just as with Lamech's corruption of the design for marriage, we also see as Genesis 4 progresses—and as Genesis as a whole progresses—how the common grace God gives to all people—the intelligence, the giftedness, the ingenuity, the opportunities—can be exploited and used in self-serving ways.

Culture-Making as Worship

Cain names the city Enoch, after his son. We might think this is a pretty sweet thing to do, but from Cain it has more of the connotation of "I made this." It is a monument to himself. (It is the seed, in fact, of the sentiment grown to full fruition in Genesis 11's Tower of Babel.)

The opportunities to leverage advances in culture and technology for the idolization of self continue today. Right here in Genesis 4:20 we see the genesis of land ownership, of expanding territories and properties, of animal husbandry and expansive livestock holdings. Then, just as today, one could acquire all of this property in an honest way, in a way that seeks the good of the land, the humane treatment of animals, the prosperity of employees and fellow workers. One could turn such wealth into a way to support ministry and mission and generations of family heirs.

Or one could acquire these things in a greedy, grubby way, in a way that exploits the land and harms it environmentally, a way that mistreats animals or causes injustice to neighbors. It may be the difference between the Bible's faithful titan of industry Job, for instance, and the modern-day Monsanto or Enron.

Right here in Genesis 4:21, we see the genesis of art culture—an art culture that can either celebrate redemption or despair; art that can highlight either bravery or debauchery; art that can either glorify God or glorify man. Then, just as today, music, paintings, and sculptures could project truth and beauty, or they could promote sin. Genesis 4:21 originates the opportunities that give rise both to Handel's *Messiah* and to Mansons Charles and Marilyn.

In Genesis 4:22 we see the genesis of industry and technology—an industrial and business culture that has provided countless outstanding advances toward our comfort and our care. Medical advances that save and prolong lives. Mechanical advances that make work and travel more efficient, home maintenance and housekeeping more effortless. Technology that makes us more intelligent, more productive, more effective. But the downsides are always there. Sin is always crouching at the door of industry and technology; its desire is for our cultural advances. So then, just as today, the same tools that can build can kill. The same technology that can save a life can harm it. The same industry that can provide employment and stability for workers can exploit them. Genesis 4:22 originates the medical advances we use to reconstruct the mouths of children born with cleft palates or provide advance prosthetics to those who've lost limbs in war or accidents—as well as those we use to provide plastic surgery for people whose vanity has overtaken their common sense.

Medical technology is used to save babies in the womb today; and it's also used to kill them. Medicine that's designed to heal illness creates illness, as it is abused into addictions. And when it comes to information technology and business, one of the fastest innovators of media content and hardware is actually the pornography industry, which drives much more of the technological culture than we realize. Advanced engineering that is used to plan cities, to build their infrastructures, is also used to destroy cities and countries. Science can help or it can hinder. Nuclear power is just one example.

Because of common grace, because humans are made in God's image, we have a great capacity for great things. You don't have to be a Christian to accomplish great things. The human race gets to enjoy all the wonders of life on this well-ordered earth, because God has made the human race smart, resourceful, resilient, and strong.

But because of the sin we've inherited from Adam, and because of the curse we and even our earth are subjected to because of that sin, we also have a great capacity for some terrible things. Both Christians and non-Christians alike. Human culture is plagued by idolatry, self-interest, and depravity of all kinds because all humans are sinners.

So even as the people of Genesis's early chapters rapidly develop culture, they are rapidly *devolving* spiritually. They are beginning the cycle of self-interest and self-exaltation that deserves the end they receive in Genesis 6, when God wipes them all out in the flood. This culminates with Lamech's song in Genesis 4:23–24:

Lamech said to his wives:

"Adah and Zillah, hear my voice;
    you wives of Lamech, listen to what I say:

> I have killed a man for wounding me,
>> a young man for striking me.
>> If Cain's revenge is sevenfold,
>>> then Lamech's is seventy-sevenfold."

What is this? Well, it's sort of like the first gangsta rap song. It is a celebration of multiple women, a celebration of violence. This song by Lamech is pure swagger and defiance. We don't know what event has occurred that he's referring to, but he's exulting in having meted out death to a young person who merely struck him. He says, "My anger, my rage, my violent vengeance is greater than my forefather Cain," which is not what you want to aspire to.

We see how easily creative and industrial aspirations turn into idolatry in an insightful passage from the prophecy of Isaiah:

> The ironsmith takes a cutting tool and works it over the coals. He fashions it with hammers and works it with his strong arm. He becomes hungry, and his strength fails; he drinks no water and is faint. The carpenter stretches a line; he marks it out with a pencil. He shapes it with planes and marks it with a compass. He shapes it into the figure of a man, with the beauty of a man, to dwell in a house. He cuts down cedars, or he chooses a cypress tree or an oak and lets it grow strong among the trees of the forest. He plants a cedar and the rain nourishes it. Then it becomes fuel for a man. He takes a part of it and warms himself; he kindles a fire and bakes bread. Also he makes a god and worships it; he makes it an idol and falls down before it. Half of it he burns in the fire. Over the half he eats meat; he roasts it and is satisfied. Also he warms himself and says, "Aha, I am warm, I have seen the fire!" And the rest of it he makes into a god, his idol, and falls down to it and worships it. He prays to it and says, "Deliver me, for you are my god!" (44:12–17)

What is happening? Men are doing what God has gifted them and called them to do. They are inventing, crafting, building, creating. The tasks described are both mundane and necessary: they are making shelter and cooking food. They are also creating art.

But something happens. And it happens quite subtly. The shift from creation of culture to creation of gods is practically seamless. It becomes, in effect, synonymous. What these men are creating could give glory to God; what they are making is not inherently *bad*. But in the end, the worship driving it all is the worship of self. Man looks at what he's created and doesn't say, "Praise be to God!" but "Praise be to me!"

What is the antidote, then? What is the story God is telling with our cultural creations and achievements? Should we, like some Christians seem to suggest, abandon "the culture" altogether?

Art's Grand Design

One of my favorite movie moments of all time is found in the 1979 film *Manhattan* where the character Isaac (played by writer/director Woody Allen) lies down on a couch contemplating his lonely existence and the despair he feels about the world. He picks up a tape recorder and speaks into it:

> Why is life worth living? It's a very good question. Um . . . well, there are certain things I guess that make it worthwhile. Like what? Okay. For me, I would say . . . Groucho Marx, to name one thing . . . and Willie Mays . . . and the second movement of the Jupiter Symphony . . . and Louis Armstrong, recording of "Potato Head Blues." Swedish movies, naturally. *Sentimental Education* by Flaubert. Marlon Brando, Frank Sinatra. Those incredible *Apples and Pears* by Cezanne. The crabs at Sam Wo's . . .

What is Isaac doing? I think he's trying to keep away the despair by reciting sources of joy, and while he does finally end his list by naming his girlfriend's face, you can see the bulk of his list consists of cultural artifacts—athletes, actors, authors, paintings, songs, and even food.

I've thought about this a lot. My list would sound something like this:

Kurosawa's *Seven Samurai*. The scene in *Casablanca* where the French drown out the Nazis singing in the Café Américain with the French anthem "La Marseillaise." The opening of Woody Allen's *Manhattan* with Gershwin's *Rhapsody in Blue* playing over a black-and-white montage of New York cityscapes. C. S. Lewis's *Perelandra*. Jonathan Edwards's "The Excellencies of Christ." Van Gogh's paintings of cypresses. Rembrandt's *Return of the Prodigal Son*. The phoenix rolls at Tokyo House in Rutland, Vermont. Charlie Peacock's "The Harvest Is the End of the World." The end of Ang Lee's *Sense and Sensibility* when Emma Thompson's Elinor finds out Hugh Grant's Edward isn't married.

I could go on and on. I ask myself, why these artifacts? What is it about them and others like them that, to use Isaac's phrase, "make life worth living"?

What is it about art—which contributes almost nothing practical to human existence (meaning, we could literally live without it)—that we can't seem to live without it?

Art is transporting. Art resonates. The best art takes some experience or moment of the world and interprets it in a way that doesn't just entertain but enlightens. When you think about it, actually, the creating of art is perhaps the closest we actually get to imaging God as Creator. When we build things that are useful, that is a kind of art, as well, and it's a way that we carry out being made in God's image, to be sure. But God did not make us or the world because he needed us. In a way, he made us because he wanted to exult in his own artistry. He wanted to convey some deeper sense of himself, to tell a story with the universe. So when we pick up a pen or paintbrush, pick away at the guitar or plink away at the piano keys, we are getting as close as mortals can get to creation *ex nihilo* ("out of nothing").

"Let there be art," we are saying, and then we make some art.

But we're all over the map with our creativity. Many use their creativity to exploit or to blaspheme. Some make art that isn't immoral, but just tacky or shallow or stupid, which is almost as bad. And yet, even in lots of popular art we can still see the themes of God's metanarrative echoing through. We can't get the image of God out of our DNA, as fallen as we are, and so we can't quite keep it out of our art either.

I will confess to being a *Taken* junkie. I love all the *Taken* movies. As I write this, I am aware of a third *Taken* film that is in post-production, and I already love it even though I haven't seen it. They can make a bunch more of these movies, and I'll watch them all, because the idea of watching Liam Neeson kicking butt and taking names while he rescues his family over and over again strikes me as both wonderfully ludicrous and deliciously *just*. Like the best works in the action/adventure genre, movies like *Taken* echo back to us a narrative theme we see in Scripture itself: conquer evil and save the girl. It's the root of every enduring fairy tale, and we find it in the great factual history of God's biblical story, throughout and in the end of which Christ defeats his enemies and rescues his bride.

You don't have to be a Christian to get this. And that's why these kinds of works resonate and endure, even the poorly made ones.

But we all know action/adventure movies can be grotesque too. They can celebrate violence for the sake of brutality itself. They can echo the classic themes of redemption and rescue, or they can merely glorify themes of bloodshed and mercilessness. I find it interesting that so many God-denying, morality-denouncing connoisseurs of art recognize depravity when they see it.

This is what film critic Roger Ebert wrote about a remake of a classic horror film:

> The new version of *The Texas Chainsaw Massacre* is a contemptible film: Vile, ugly and brutal. There is not a shred of a reason to see it. Those who defend it will have to dance through mental hoops of their own devising, defining its meanness and despair as "style" or "vision" or "a commentary on our world." It is not a commentary on anything, except the marriage of slick technology with the materials of a geek show.[1]

---

[1] Roger Ebert, "The Texas Chainsaw Massacre," *RogerEbert.com*, October 17, 2003, http://www.rogerebert.com/reviews/the-texas-chainsaw-massacre-2003/.

Roger Ebert until his death maintained both an uneasy affection for his Roman Catholic upbringing and a decided personal affiliation with atheism. And yet of all the secular film critics I'm familiar with, he seemed the most comfortable making moral evaluations of the movies he reviewed. Make no mistake: he is saying here that *The Texas Chainsaw Massacre* is an immoral film. And not because it was a horror movie. Ebert liked plenty of those. Not because it was a popular-level entry in the world of cinema. Ebert appreciated plenty of mainstream films. He didn't even speak of it this way because it was a poorly made movie. He had no trouble saying such things when the entry warranted them.[2]

No, he called it immoral because it communicated despair and brutality in a way that glorified despair and brutality. It was, in the parlance of today's cinema critics, "torture porn." And if an atheist like Roger Ebert has no problem calling torture porn immoral, we should be emboldened to join him in admitting that there are works of art that might be made well but communicate unworthy ideas, just like there may be works of art that communicate worthy ideas that undercut themselves by being poorly made.

Remember that a work of art is not about what it's about; it's about *how* it is about it. What I mean is, a work of art is not bad simply because it carries as its subject things that are bad—sexual immorality, murder, greed, or the like. A work of art would be immoral if it glorified or promoted such things. But simply to discuss them is not in itself bad; otherwise, we'd have to categorize much of the Old Testament as immoral.

I remember watching a movie from director Sofia Coppola called *The Bling Ring*, ostensibly a stolen-from-the-headlines story about a group of spoiled Hollywood brats who, jealous of the celebrity life, begin robbing the homes of famous starlets like Kim Kardashian and Paris Hilton. The movie itself was pretty unremarkable. It was boring, actually. But I watched the whole thing and while at first I was a little confused as to why Coppola would depict

---

[2] See Roger Ebert, *Your Movie Sucks* (New York: Andrews McMeel, 2007).

such deliriously fame-hungry thieves carrying out such daring capers in such a mundane way, it occurred to me that that might be her whole point! These are boring people. Their values are boring. Their motivations are boring. Their thoughts are boring. Even the targets of their envy and their crimes are boring. In her own stylized way, Coppola was putting this kind of behavior in its proper moral light. It didn't make the movie itself better, but it certainly made it more a work of art. I imagined what the movie would've been like if Michael Bay had directed it. It gave me a greater appreciation for what Coppola was saying.

The world has already pretty much forgotten *The Bling Ring*—both the movie and the real-life nitwits who inspired it—but the kind of art the world will remember long after its creation is art that not only says something but that taps into the grand themes present in the big story God is telling with the universe. This is why both action movies and romantic comedies are so popular. And it's why works like *Les Miserables* and *Crime and Punishment* and *The Odyssey* endure so long. They rehearse in some way the moral framework of God's creative universe and echo the storyline of Creation, Fall, Redemption, and Restoration.

But these works do so in such a way that communicates in both message *and tone*. It is not enough to simply say the right things, as important as that is. We must say them in the right ways, which is to say, with excellence, with gravity, and with grace—in short, with artistry! This is why so much so-called "Christian art" fails. It very often says the right thing but in rather unartful ways. At best, such artifacts are simply propaganda. At worst, they effectively work against the message they are trying to convey.

When God looks over his creation and says, "It is good," he doesn't just mean that it's good he made all that stuff. That's definitely true. But he also means, "I made good stuff." He's saying, "I made this well."

Human beings, for instance, aren't just made; they are "fearfully and wonderfully made" (Ps. 139:14).

When we approach art from this perspective, we give more glory to God than when we come at art just for passive entertainment. And when our talented artists seek to create their work conscious of the deeper truth of God's artistry, they understand that writing books and poetry, composing songs, snapping pictures, filming movies, shaping sculptures, and painting portraits all to the glory of God mean both communicating truth (even if implicitly) and conveying glory. This means adorning the truth with beauty and thoughtfulness.

In chapter 3, I referenced C. S. Lewis's great line about myth in his science-fiction novel *Perelandra*. The character Ransom realizes that myth is simply "beams of celestial beauty falling on a jungle of filth and imbecility." This, in short, is what good art is. Art is not good if it is popular or high-brow, if it is of one particular medium or genre or another. Art is good if it in some way offers a glimpse into the beauty and glory of God and his ways through the interpreting of the stuff of earth.

The heavens declare the glory of God, but not because you can read Bible verses in the clouds. In the same way, the best art communicates on a deeper level the kinds of truth embedded in the world that is groaning for redemption and in the fallen men and women who are made in God's image.

Now we've got our pink and brown pieces of the pie. On to that pesky green category.

Science Fictions

One of today's cultural hot topics is the supposed irreconcilable difference between science and religion. Fortunately, some of our earliest Christian forefathers saw no tension between the two.

We could start with the New Testament's own beloved physician Luke the Evangelist, who turned his surgical precision not just to medicine but to the historical record of Jesus and his apostles in the Gospel named after him and the book called Acts. But we also have men like Bede, a monk who as early as the seventh century was writing about the nature of time and the phenomenon of tides. Nemesius was a bishop in the fourth century who studied the brain. The earliest astronomers, medical doctors, and mathematicians were generally all men who believed in the Creator God. Modern thinkers sometimes laugh at their scientific conclusions as much as their religious ones, but their efforts could not be said to be incompatible with their faith. In the minds of such Christian thinkers, yesterday and today, God has made a finely tuned, deeply complex, and incredibly beautiful universe. Why wouldn't we want to dig in?

Today, of course, science is often replaced by scientism, wherein the study of the universe becomes an end in and of itself. Interestingly, we see the problem with this approach in some of our most finely tuned works of art. Stanley Kubrick's *2001: A Space Odyssey* is one example. The film follows the themes of exploration, discovery, and man's origins and meaning. As excellently as the movie is made, Kubrick has nonetheless made a cold film. It is haunting, it is awesome, it is overwhelming. But it nonetheless gives the feeling of emptiness, of despair. It is as if Kubrick (adapting an Arthur C. Clarke novel) knows that man's search for meaning lies somewhere "out there," and outer space is the only setting boundless, uncontrollable, and epic enough to get at whatever that meaning might be, but in the end he still only finds the search. The protagonist, astronaut David Bowman, is transformed in the end of the film into a sort of galactic space-fetus, orbiting the earth in an orb of energy. The movie appears to say that the search—the gaze—is all there is.

Others, however, see in the pursuit of space—or the deep sea, the "God particle," that theory of everything—an opportunity to reveal the bottomless well of God's glory embedded in creation.

When we put scientific research to use in service of God's glory, we find new ways to explore his intricate world and new ways to leverage the glory embedded in creation toward consolation of the fallenness in creation. That's the kind of scientific pursuit that taps into the story God is telling with the gospel.

Science gives us medicine, antidotes, therapy, and prosthetics.

Scientific study is helping us unlock the mysteries of the brain and the rest of our bodies, that we might be able to "do no harm." But this kind of pursuit has turned in on itself. As our works of culture drift, drift, drift into idolatries of all kinds, we make a scientific discovery and lean back, beaming, "Deliver me, for you are my god!"

With this kind of spiritual dullness in the heart, no amount of scientific intelligence can save us. So now we employ our brightest minds in the abortion and euthanasia of the defenseless, and the exploitation and obliteration of our enemies.

The stories we try to tell with our self-reverential intelligence today are science fictions. Some scientists imagine that with all the good they do—and all genuine scientific good gives God glory, whether it is carried out by God-worshipers or not—they justify the divorce between science and religion. But they have really only served a religion of another kind. Science becomes its own religion. Would that more scientists seeking the key to human longevity (immortality?) might take to heart the poetic formula of C. T. Studd: "Only *one life*, 'twill soon be *past*; only what's done for Christ will last."

The story God is telling with the world of science fits neatly into the story he is telling with human society and culture in general. It is meant to reveal that we are broken because of sin and in need of redemption by glory. So when scientists follow the evidence like crumbs leading to the Bread of Life, they are on the right track. When we comfort, heal, fix, and restore, we employ our intelligence in testimony to Christ's work of making all things new. Scientific discoveries and revelations can become wonderful parables of the day when there will be no more sickness, disease, pain, or even death.

But when our culture denies and suppresses what the world around us is constantly declaring, we are headed for disaster. There's no tower we can build so big that God won't still have to come down from heaven to snicker at it.

We must keep this humbling truth in mind not just when contemplating the big worlds of art and science, however, but in the everyday world of coffee and computers and carpooling.

Working for Somebody Else's Living

Let's revisit God's mandate to Adam and Eve: "Be fruitful and multiply and fill the earth and subdue it, and have dominion" (Gen. 1:28). In this commandment is the multifaceted call to build civilization, create culture, make art. Adam and Eve are told to learn, to construct, to organize. In this one verse lies the essence of the Christian doctrine of vocation.

The idea of vocation is sorely needed in the Christian culture today, because many of us still tend to think in *overly* religious ways about our purpose in the world. We tend to draw very stark lines between the spiritual and the earthly, between the explicitly religious and the immediately practical. Many Christians struggle with understanding how going to their "secular" jobs each day—or staying home to tend house—has any kind of meaning in the scope of eternity. But as we have established, Jesus is making all things new, and God has called us to give glory to him in all of those things, so the doctrine of vocation helps us understand what difference making copies and making coffee makes.

Since we spend so much of our lives doing these things that are not explicitly spiritual, it behooves us to understand how we might search for connection and significance in them, rather than around them. We tend to compartmentalize our lives, assuming the spiritual part of us must be crammed into the margins of our work week, where we might pursue religion or theology. But God has designed the idea of work itself to contribute to the story he is telling with the universe.

Still, even for the irreligious, the desire to find connection and significance in our everyday, workaday lives is undeniable. And like the idolatrous culture-makers of Isaiah 44, we follow this desire not to the Giver of all good things but back into ourselves. So we make a substitute religion out of the entire enterprise. We cast it into the ambition of something greater, beyond ourselves. But it is still something that falls short of God's glory. Sometimes we call this substitute religion the American Dream.

Now, some aspects of what we call the American Dream are not incompatible with Christian living. Things like getting married, starting a family, pursuing a successful career, putting down roots, creating financial stability and security for your loved ones, and even creating jobs and opportunities for others in your life and community can be distinctly Christian things. These are ordinary, honorable ways we love our neighbors just as God commanded us. But what the American Dream has come to symbolize in an idolatrous culture—pursuit of wealth, material goods, success through excess and conspicuous consumption—is completely antithetical to the call of Christ to the kingdom of God.

The story of the American Dream, if we are not sober-minded about the world and focused on God's story, becomes about laying up treasures on earth. Jesus says some hard words about that kind of investment (Matt. 6:19–20; Mark 8:36; 10:23).

And yet, as Martin Luther says, there is a great danger of falling off the horse on the other side.[3] The biblical response to materialism is not Gnosticism—a way of thinking that assumes material or earthly things are inherently bad—or hyperspiritual abstention from the world, but instead a Christ-centered investment in the world that serves the joy of others as much as ourselves.

As the gospel takes dominion in our lives, it will eventually spill over into our areas of responsibility and influence outside the home. At work, at school, and in our neighborly "third places" (the social environments we spend time in between home and work), what God's story gives us is a new view of vocation, where our activity outside the home is not merely duty but delight, an expression of worship in testimony to God's goodness and glory.

---

[3] Martin Luther, "Andere Fabeln, Gleichnisse, Bilder und Ahnliches, 19, Der Welt Bild" in *Martin Luther: ausgewahlt, bearbeitet un erlautert von Richard Neubauer* (Halle: Waisenhaus, 1890–1891), 2:115. Quoted in Ludwig Feuerbach, *Abelard and Heloise, or: The Writer and the Human* (North Syracuse, New York: Gegensatz Press, 2012), 73.

Let's look at a famous passage from the prophet Jeremiah's book. Within this passage we find one of the most quoted verses in all evangelicalism: Jeremiah 29:11. What we do with Jeremiah 29:11 often feeds right back into the kind of self-interested ambition that God's story is meant to deliver us from. So as we look at the context, let's see what God has called his worshipers to actually do *as* a culture *in* the culture.

The prophecy in view begins like this: "Thus says the LORD of hosts, the God of Israel, to all the exiles whom I have sent into exile from Jerusalem to Babylon" (29:4).

The situation for the children of Israel is parallel to the situation the church finds itself in today. That situation is called *exile*.

Exile presupposes that we are in Babylon, not Jerusalem. So one of the major mistakes the church has made is expecting Babylon to act like Jerusalem, to be like Jerusalem, to recognize Jerusalem as an ideal. We see this in the way Christians keep trying to convince non-Christians that America is really a Christian nation and needs to start acting like it again.

The church's missional posture has reflected this expectation.

But the reality is that we should not expect Babylon to start acting like Jerusalem. The church should instead live like Jerusalem within Babylon (Matt. 5:14; John 17:14–19). Here are the instructions to the children of Israel in the midst of their exile:

> Build houses and live in them; plant gardens and eat their produce. Take wives and have sons and daughters; take wives for your sons, and give your daughters in marriage, that they may bear sons and daughters; multiply there, and do not decrease. (Jer. 29:5–6)

First of all, does any of this give the sense of "just passing through"? Does it look temporary? Does this give the impression that God's people are to live like this place was not their home?

"This world is not my home." It's a popular phrase in the lexicon of Christianese, and there is a sense in which it's true. But, as the very premise of this book is meant to demonstrate, there is a sense in which it is not.

When we say things like "this world is not my home," we should *not* mean that this world is not the place God has called us to live out his kingdom. I mean, here we are. Where else are we going to live? The biblical forecast of the new heavens and new earth shows us that this world *is* our home—at least, the transformed version of it that is still to come.

When we say, "This world is not my home," we should mean the world that is passing away—the sinful system of the world, the corruption, the injustice. In other words, suburbia may be your home, but consumerism should not be. America may be your home, but idolatrous nationalism should not be. Your nice house may be your home, but Christ alone should be your security.

On the other hand, if we think only in short-term ways about the world around us, we may become careless and negligent in loving our neighbors. We see this sometimes in the ways American Christians buy into the worldly ethos of convenience and comfort, of living at the expense of others. Some treat the environment recklessly, assuming it's all going to burn up anyway.

But God calls us to a better way: Not to be so heavenly minded that we're no earthly good, but also not to be so earthly minded that we're no heavenly good. Instead, Jeremiah 29:5–6 urges us to *live invested*.

The themes of Jeremiah 29:5–6 are similar to the aims of the American Dream, but the focus of the biblical investment that God calls the exiles to is not on their own peace and prosperity but on that of their neighbors. Therefore: "But seek the welfare of the city where I have sent you into exile, and pray to the LORD on its behalf, for in its welfare you will find your welfare" (29:7).

Now here is something really unique! A Jerusalem that is *for* Babylon. A community centered on God that is *for* the community centered on itself. Or, to use the parlance of today's church planting movement, "a city for the city."

Jeremiah 29:7 shows us "love your neighbor" on the missio-
logical scale. If you want to prosper, God says, you will seek the
prospering of your neighbors.

We contrast this with the two primary ways Christians relate to
the world around them: as consumers and as combatants.

In the consumeristic mode, we end up using the community for
our comfort and convenience. We are aimed at our own prosperity not by the prosperity of our neighbors but around it. For the
consumeristic church, the world exists to be used, consumed, and
profited from.

In combat mode, we engage in full-on culture war. We lambast
our enemies, ridicule them, shame them, and seek to marginalize
or demoralize them through the sheer force of our rhetoric or our
legislation or our numbers or our voice.

Why do we act like that? Jeremiah 29:8–9 says it's because we
believe in lies:

> For thus says the LORD of hosts, the God of Israel: Do not let
> your prophets and your diviners who are among you deceive
> you, and do not listen to the dreams that they dream, for it is a
> lie that they are prophesying to you in my *name; I did not send
> them, declares the* LORD.

False prophets lead us astray. We listen and believe lies from
within the camp and lies from outside. Lies from within sound like
this:

"If we just had the right person in the White House . . ."
"If we just got the right laws in place . . ."
"If we just got prayer back in schools . . ."
Lies from without sound like this:
"Get more, be more, do more."
"He who dies with the most toys wins."
We buy into these lies and bring them into the camp and de-
Christ our Christianity with them. Simply put, the world does not
need more combatants and consumers. It needs Christians. It needs

Christians who will commit to "living invested" in the Jeremiah 29 sense while doing essentially three things:

We need to exegete our communities. When Paul entered Athens, he saw that the city was full of idols (Acts 17:16). It is important to interpret our communities by understanding the motivations and appetites and wounds beneath the symptoms, the sins beneath the sins as it were. Identifying idols is important because it prevents us from falling sway to them ourselves, and it helps us actually help people with solutions they need.

We need to love our communities. You cannot love somebody and use them at the same time. When Christ saw the crowd of sinners around him, he did not turn up his nose in disgust; he did not put together a petition or a picket line. Instead, he saw them as lost sheep, hurt and harassed, and he had compassion. To love our neighbors means sacrificially serving them, and it means doing so in primarily this way:

We need to proclaim Christ in our communities. Christians exegete their communities, love their communities, and proclaim Christ in their communities. We bear witness with our words and deeds to what we believe about this world, what we believe about this nation of ours. Some Christians believe in America so much that it is clear where their belief really lies: America. But it is Christ who is King, it is Christ who is God, it is Christ who is our only hope. And God's plan for the world, America included, is to saturate every nook and cranny, every deep sea trench, and every highest mountain peak with the radiance of his glory. Let *that* be our dream.

Now, we take these tasks into the world as our primary mission: to give God glory through bearing with our coworkers or our fellow students or the PTA or the HOA in an understanding way, seeing them all as people made by God after his own image, and sharing the love of Christ with them in humble, loving, edifying ways.

For the children of Israel in Babylonian exile, the forecasted result of their investment is breathtaking:

> For thus says the LORD: When seventy years are completed
> for Babylon, I will visit you, and I will fulfill to you my prom-
> ise and bring you back to this place. For I know the plans I
> have for you, declares the LORD, plans for welfare and not for
> evil, to give you a future and a hope. Then you will call upon
> me and come and pray to me, and I will hear you. You will
> seek me and find me, when you seek me with all your heart.
> I will be found by you, declares the LORD, and I will restore
> your fortunes and gather you from all the nations and all the
> places where I have driven you, declares the LORD, and I will
> bring you back to the place from which I sent you into exile.
> (Jer. 29:10–14)

Here we find our famous verse. It's one we realize is for us and
therefore make about us. But Jeremiah 29:11 is only about getting
what you want if what you want is Christ.

No, the gospel is not completely incompatible with some aspects
of the American Dream, especially as it relates to providing for
our families, seeking the good of our fellow citizens, and providing
jobs, and therefore flourishing our neighbors. But the gospel is very
much against the prevailing mythos of the American Dream because
the gospel seeks to galvanize our affections toward the only One
worthy of them.

As we live invested in our communities, let us decrease that
Christ may increase. This is the essence of the doctrine of vocation. It is the way we participate in and contribute to (influence!)
our culture. Let us be joyful exiles, pointing with our very lives to
the great story of redemption and restoration God is telling by the
gospel in the very context of our neighborhoods and workplaces.

Can you imagine what it will be like to work and do business
in the new heavens and new earth? There will be no more greed,
no more injustice, no more gluttony, no more thievery, no more
fatigue, no more corruption. Knowing all this, how might we do
business and even do life in a way that communicates we believe in
the age to come?

Remembering Our Place in the Story

I have a friend who says he feels like Gulliver, tied down by millions of tiny strings. One or two, or even twenty, might not be such a big deal. He could move around plenty. But all together, he feels stifled. He's asking the right question, I think.

"How do I start cutting strings?"

His self-reflection encourages and challenges me. Over time, reflexively accumulating the expectations of what it means to grow up and create "a life" for yourself, your family, and your future, we submit to strings upon strings. There comes a day many wake up and realize they're suffocating.

I think of the early retiree with lots of money saved up in the bank and plenty of time for boating and golfing. He is finally getting to do all the time what he never had much time for but most enjoyed while he was working. Focused only on his own pleasure, he is still wasting his life.

We're told to save, get our kids in the right schools and extra-curriculars, get the right insurance, build equity, invest in college savings programs and retirement accounts, succeed in business. Our churches know these are priorities, so they tell us how to put the Bible's principles to work so we'll have successful marriages, jobs, families, businesses, lives.

This is laying up treasures on earth.

I don't think this is the legacy we're meant to create. Telling the story of the indomitable human spirit and the triumph of man over adversity is not the best use of our lives. Because the hero of so many of our life stories is us, our life stories are not redemptive. They don't glisten with eternity.

In Haggai 1:4 the Lord rebukes the nation of Israel: "Is it a time for you yourselves to be living in your paneled houses, while this house remains a ruin?" (NIV).

We don't have to rebuild the temple, of course. But the church in the West is full of Christians who have bought into with heart, mind, and soul the pursuit of erecting houses of worship of the human spirit. The world around us bids us build monuments to ourselves and our ingenuity and perseverance. And the dying Servant-King bids us come and die. "Is it a time for you yourselves to be living in your tidy, safe, comfortable, successful, consumeristic, materialistic lives while the kingdom goes ignored?"

Let us remember the pronouncement of our Author: "For you are dust, and to dust you shall return" (Gen. 3:19). How does *that* affect your sense of vocation? It certainly flies in the face of the man-exalting stories we try to live out.

I have a problem with all the "chase your dreams!" cheerleading from Christian leaders. It's not because I begrudge people who want to achieve their dreams, but because I think we don't readily see how easy it is to conflate our dream-chasing with God's will in Christ. You know, it's possible that God's plan for us is littleness. His plan for us may be personal failure. It's possible that when another door closes, it's not because he plans to open a window but because he plans to have the building fall down on you. The question we must ask ourselves is this: Will Christ be enough?

Are we pursuing our own greatness or the expansion of worship of Jesus Christ? They aren't necessarily incompatible, but God is more interested in the latter than the former. And ultimately, if we prioritize Christ's glory, we won't really care in the long run how noticed, renowned, recognized, or successful we are personally. We won't care about making a name for ourselves. We'll realize that our lives aren't really about us anyway, that the story of creation is not about us at all.

Does our cultural engagement speak to this vital reality? That God is the point of human existence? That God is the point of art and science and work and everything else?

And lest we think this is really a raw deal for us, we ought to remember that the gospel that proclaims God's glory in Christ does so precisely through our redemption in Christ. The story is not about us, but it is *for* us! Therefore, if we are bringing glory to Jesus, not a thing about us is wasted, because the mission of the Spirit of God is to maximize the glory of Christ over all the universe.

At the end of days, as Revelation 21 suggests, all the titans of industry among the nations, from the richest CEO to the humblest custodians, the cubicle jockeys, and the stay-at-home moms, will file one by one into the holy city to throw their crowns at the feet of Jesus. That is God's plan for culture—that he would increase and we would decrease. That our decrease would *serve* his increase!

And those who are willing to lose their lives—whatever that might mean—for Christ's sake, will find them.

And *from* dust they will return.

6

And Justice for All

God's Plan for Evil

I watched the plane crash into the second tower live on television while holding my three-month-old daughter in my lap.

I was doing my morning routine, sitting in the bed giving the baby her bottle while watching the *Today* show. I have no idea what the scheduled segment had been. All I remember was the coverage switching over to the sight of the World Trade Center, where the North Tower had a gaping, smoking hole in it. Matt Lauer was relaying reports of a plane crash, and from the images and the reporting, the assumption was that a small plane had accidentally collided with the tower. But as the camera held its gaze on the crash scene, another plane came into view. I thought to myself, "That seems low."

Then United Airlines Flight 175 slammed into the South Tower, sending an explosion of fire and debris into the air. You've seen the footage, and whether you saw it live or recorded, I'm sure you felt the same sense of dread I felt.

I looked down at Macy, my firstborn, eyes closed and peacefully sighing in slumber. I thought, "What kind of world did we just bring you into?"

At that moment, I thought we were being invaded. There was no telling what the future would look like as reports followed of more planes crashing (into the Pentagon, into a field in Pennsylvania). In the ensuing months we had anthrax scares and sniper attacks. My wife Becky worked at a fairly large company that was receiving white powder in the mail, prompting several evacuations and quarantines.

Watching our little girl get bigger, eat her first solid food, take her first steps, say her first words, I was afraid of the brokenness she was growing up into.

See, 9/11 was supposed to change America. Of course, it did. I remember how in the immediate aftermath people flocked to churches for answers and the entertainment media wrung their hands about whether they could make jokes now or make violent movies now. People banded together across many cultural divides; we felt victimized together, we felt violated together, we felt patriotic together. Many tribute songs were sung. Many think pieces were written. And over a decade later, we haven't forgotten. And yet, we did kind of go back to business as usual. The only thing that's really changed is that we are more paranoid now and more watched by our government. But violence goes on unabated. Irreverent humor is more popular than ever.

9/11 did not wake us up from our spiritual stupor. It only disrupted it for a moment. Once the smoke cleared, we went right back to shaking our fists at God. The shock of the evil perpetrated against us wore off, so we went back to yawning at the evil all around us. And we will keep doing that until another irruption of the real occurs.

It has always been like this.

There Never Was a Golden Age

When a white Missouri police officer named Darren Wilson shot and killed a young black man named Michael Brown on August 9, 2014, African Americans everywhere thought, "It has always been like this."

The killing in the streets of Ferguson, a neighboring city to St. Louis, sparked another national conversation about race and rights. It is not an exaggeration to say that in the days and weeks after Brown's death, the way one interpreted the alleged events of the moments leading up to the shooting largely depended on one's race. Whites tended to read the shooting differently than blacks. Whether you assumed Wilson feared for his life and fired in self-defense or he callously murdered Brown in cold blood probably had a lot to do with how you normally experience the police. If you're white, you probably tend to view police corruption as exceedingly rare. You know it exists, but you do not tend to distrust law enforcement. If you're black, you likely believe that there are lots of good police officers out there, but the historic relationship between law enforcement and your people makes you incredibly uneasy. Even if you have not experienced firsthand what it's like to be followed around in a store, pulled over in traffic, or generally looked down upon by the police for no apparent reason, chances are very good that you are closely related to those who have.

As tragic as the killing of Brown is, and while we may never know what really happened that day (witness reports conflict and the autopsy results do not rule out either murder or self-defense), the stark contrast between most whites and most blacks in response to the tragedy is important and valuable to note. It reminds us that our world—that our *history*—is broken.

I try to bring this to mind when I hear white Christians waxing poetic about the good ol' days. "If only we could go back," they say. "Back to the days of Mayberry. Back to the days of *Leave It to Beaver*. Back to the days of prayer in schools. When you could walk down the street in safety."

I want to say to such memory minders, "You mean, back to the days of segregation? Water fountains for 'colored' folk? Back when prayer was in white schools but blacks weren't?"

The reality is that every golden age for one culture was an age of oppression and marginalization for another. There simply is no such thing as a golden age. Since the fall of mankind, every minute of every age has been infected by sin and thus impacted by brokenness, injustice, and oppression.

We ought to do away with our tidy utopian histories. Every human age is fraught with evil.

It did not take long for the original sin of mankind to take root and bear rotten fruit. We have already seen how the sin of Adam and Eve created division not just between them and God but between themselves. And even as they took up God's mandate to be fruitful and multiply, even as mankind progresses under God's call to subdue the earth and have dominion, the division widens and deepens. The original disobedience broke the world. And all of mankind's building has not stopped the breaking.

We have seen how sin infected the first family. We have seen how it infected the first city. We have seen how it infected the first cultures and constructions. So long as men multiply, so will sin. And when we are not deep into God's story, we see just how awful this infection has spread.

> When man began to multiply on the face of the land and daughters were born to them, the sons of God saw that the daughters of man were attractive. And they took as their wives any they chose. Then the LORD said, "My Spirit shall not abide in man forever, for he is flesh: his days shall be 120 years." The Nephilim were on the earth in those days, and also afterward, when the sons of God came in to the daughters of man and they bore children to them. These were the mighty men who were of old, the men of renown.
>
> The LORD saw that the wickedness of man was great in the earth, and that every intention of the thoughts of his heart was only evil continually. And the LORD regretted that he had made man on the earth, and it grieved him to his heart. So the LORD said, "I will blot out man whom I have created from the face of the land, man and animals and creeping things and birds of the heavens, for I am sorry that I have made them." (Gen. 6:1–7)

In Genesis 6, the depravity of the human spirit is having systemic, even biological effects. From this moment on, the lifespan of men steadily declines. Like Adam and Eve before them, every human has reached for immortality. Pride has taken over them in such a way that they think they're invincible. So God cuts them short. This is described as a sort of taking his Spirit from them (v. 3).

I do think there are times in our culture when sin has become so systemic that God in a sense hands us over to ourselves. We see this explicitly discussed in Romans 1:

> "Therefore God gave them up in the lusts of their hearts to impurity" (v. 24).

> "God gave them up to dishonorable passions" (v. 26).

> "Since they did not see fit to acknowledge God, God gave them up to a debased mind to do what ought not to be done" (v. 28).

That's what's taking place in Genesis 6:5: "The LORD saw that the wickedness of man was great in the earth, and that every intention of the thoughts of his heart was only evil continually."

It's a scary thing, to be given up by God to our sin.

In this historical scene, he does this in response to a particular lifestyle epidemic.

God's people are embracing the depravity of the ungodly. The godly begin to take wives from the ungodly simply because they were "attractive." *Nephilim* literally means "fallen ones" or "ones who fall." These Nephilim are likely the product of the intermarriage of the Sethite line and Cainite line from Adam.

But we get the sense as this passage develops that the Nephilim are not a special breed of person, really, but a *type* of person: violent, crude, sexually immoral. The sense of "fallenness" is about both their fallen nature and the way they treat others. Martin Luther interpreted Nephilim as tyrants, because they are largely characterized by oppression.

Nephilim were very influential, very infamous, very mean and corrupt and tyrannical people. This seems likely because the passage says they were around before the intermarriage (which would, I think, rule out the theory that they were products of demon-human interbreeding) and they were around after intermarriage. In other words, the emphasis in this passage—and the emphasis throughout the sordid family history of Genesis on through the rest of the Pentateuch—is not really about preserving a race, but preserving the faith.

In any event, the result of this ungodly pairing is an entire culture of depraved rebels. God takes one look at the whole mess and is offended. He even says he's "sorry" that he made man.

Now, God had not done anything wrong. He made creation good. And he knew full well when he created Adam and Eve that their virtue wouldn't last. We have to be careful with the word *regret* in Genesis 6:6. First Samuel 15:29 says, "And also the Glory of Israel will not lie or have regret, for he is not a man, that he should have regret." No, verse 6's *regret* is in tension with "grieved to his heart."

Sin so grieves the God of creation that he cannot turn a blind eye to it. He must execute judgment, because his glory is at stake. And in fact, we see his glory in his vengeance, because it is through God's wrath for sin that we feel the gravity of his holiness and his righteousness and his justice.

Genesis 6:5 is devastating: "The LORD saw that the wickedness of man was great in the earth, and that every intention of the thoughts of his heart was only evil continually." And verse 7 is terrifying: "So the LORD said, 'I will blot out man whom I have created from the face of the land.'"

You know what happens next. God tells Noah—who, by the way, is not a sinless person—to build an ark. And then God sends a flood to wipe out everyone and everything but Noah and his family.

Noah found favor in God's eyes (6:8). But because the flood did not wipe out Noah and his family, it also did not wipe out sin.

Why We Can't Get It Right

The reason God spared Noah and his family was not because they were sinless paragons of virtue. By wrathfully and graciously re-booting civilization, God was not trying to re-create Eden.

So when the waters recede, and Noah and kin come out of the ark, sin comes out with them. In fact, the curious episode in Genesis 9 involving Noah's son taking advantage of his drunk father is the earliest proof of that. Try as we may, we can't get the "acting right" thing right. Because we are fallen creatures, we just keep falling. As Paul writes in Romans 8:20, "The creation was subjected to futility."

We like our gods holy. You don't even have to be religious to fall into this trap. Over and over again, we find both surprise and then dismissal when our cultural heroes and leaders reveal their fallen-ness. Presidents Kennedy and Clinton are revealed to be adulterers. Ditto Martin Luther King Jr. Mahatma Ghandi liked sharing his bed with multiple women too. Most of our founding fathers were slave owners.

The Mormons recently admitted, after many long years of public denial, that their founder Joseph Smith was a polygamist. Histori-ans have well documented Smith's appetites for wifely accumula-tion, including underage girls. But the Mormon authorities, fearing the PR troubles for the institution, kept denouncing the evidence as smear campaigns and bad history. They finally now admit what most religious scholars already knew, although they spin it to say Smith didn't want to marry multiple wives and only did so under angelic coercion.

Christian heroes do not escape the indictment. Throughout church history, many of our towering figures were anti-Semites, harsh husbands, and heretic killers. Some were given to too much drink or too much anger.

Our biblical heroes are a mixed bag too.

We like to make excuses for all of these people. Their good outweighs their bad, we want to argue. We dismiss the sins of our heroes, because deep down we do not like what it might say about us. If these great men and women struggled so badly, what might be made of us lesser men and women?

There was only one sinless man to walk the earth. "All have sinned and fall short of the glory of God" (Rom. 3:23). No matter how hard we try, no matter how well we spin, no matter how neatly we dismiss—the sin remains.

Paul explains the mess better than anybody:

> For I do not understand my own actions. For I do not do what I want, but I do the very thing I hate. Now if I do what I do not want, I agree with the law, that it is good. So now it is no longer I who do it, but sin that dwells within me. For I know that nothing good dwells in me, that is, in my flesh. For I have the desire to do what is right, but not the ability to carry it out. For I do not do the good I want, but the evil I do not want is what I keep on doing. Now if I do what I do not want, it is no longer I who do it, but sin that dwells within me.
>
> So I find it to be a law that when I want to do right, evil lies close at hand. For I delight in the law of God, in my inner being, but I see in my members another law waging war against the law of my mind and making me captive to the law of sin that dwells in my members. Wretched man that I am! Who will deliver me from this body of death? (Rom. 7:15–24)

What Paul is describing is the spiritual reality of the war-torn soul *of the believer in Christ*. His spirit is willing, but his flesh is weak. He knows the good to do, but he can't do it perfectly. He knows the bad to avoid, but he can't stay away completely. It is even more difficult for those who do not have the Holy Spirit living within them, even for those who are consciously trying to be good people.

We can't get this right. We never have. And we never will. This has been true of both Adolf Hitler and Mother Theresa. This is true of you and me. Evil, as the Lord says to Cain, crouches right outside our doors. It would have us. And we would have it.

It doesn't even matter if you're not a murderer. If you've hated, you're just as guilty on your own (Matt. 5:21–22). It doesn't matter if you've never cheated on your spouse. If you've lusted, you're just as guilty (5:27–28). There may be big sins and little sins as they relate to earthly consequences, but one sin is enough to deserve the wrath of a holy God. Do you imagine that everybody who was wiped out by the flood was an Adolf Hitler?

We can't conquer evil on our own. It's real; it exists. And it's too much for us. We can restrain it in many ways. We can denounce it. We can pass laws, carry out executions. But so long as there are sinners in the world, there will be evil in the world.

But there won't always be sinners in the world.

Evil's Expiration Date

It was Saturday, December 15, 2012, and I faced a dilemma. The next morning I was scheduled to preach another entry in our church's sermon series through the Gospel of Mark. But the day before, a young man named Adam Lanza had gone into the elementary school near his home and murdered twenty-six people, twenty of whom were kindergarten students. The nation was stunned.

Sadly, school shootings seem to have become more commonplace in our country. I can vividly remember the apparent watershed event of the Columbine High School massacre in 1999, but these killings in Newtown, Connecticut, became the deadliest grade school mass shooting in United States history. The idea of Lanza murdering twenty five- and six-year-olds one by one was (and is) chilling.

On that Saturday I contemplated preaching in response to the murders. I had never done such a thing. In theory, I have always been opposed to letting the latest headlines drive my preaching schedule. It is one reason why I like preaching through books of the Bible and why I like to schedule my sermons out six months at a time. But this event seemed too big, too dark not to say something. If another 9/11 had occurred, I would have felt prompted to speak on God's behalf to my flock about it. I don't need to tune my sermons to the weekly news cycle, but when evil strikes so vividly and so close to home (Newtown is only three-and-a-half hours from our home in Vermont), I think there may be an obligation to address it beyond a sound bite. Nonetheless, I wrestled with my decision all day Saturday and never quite felt at peace about it until Sunday morning, when I finally decided to scrap my planned sermon and write a new one.

At five o'clock that Sunday morning I sat at the table by our picture window and prayed and stared at the blinking cursor on my laptop and asked, "What would God say about Newtown?"

What I was really asking is what people have been asking since evil began: "How long, O Lord?" It is the cry resounding throughout the Psalms and the Prophets. How long will God let evil exist? How long will he let it increase? How long will he let man fall victim to man? What is he going to do about all the evil in the world?

If Noah's story tells us anything, it tells us that God has a vested stake in his creation and the creatures in it, and that God is not ambivalent or apathetic about sin. He must and will do something about it. He "will by no means clear the guilty" (Ex. 34:7).

And though punishment seems to delay—we hate this about our enemies but certainly appreciate it for our own sake!—we also see in Noah's story what the righteous do in the meantime. Hebrews 11:7 tells us that it was "by faith" that Noah built the ark, and I imagine it would have had to have been by faith because, assuming it took anywhere from seventy-five to a hundred years to build the thing, all along he had to trust that just because God wasn't doing something *yet* didn't mean he wasn't going to do something.

I imagine that while Noah was building this ark, the people of his day might have stopped by to snicker. Maybe hold out their hands to feel for rain in mockery. Maybe, like today's mockers of the godly, they suggested Noah was wasting his life on superstitious myths. If these events were taking place today, they'd say with much pity and condescension that Noah was a member of the flat earth society. The world has moved on from belief in impulsive ghosts in the sky who control things.

And this *is* happening today. Today the worldly mockers surround the faithful builders of God's kingdom of righteousness and say, "Hey, news flash: The culture war is over and you lost. You are on the wrong side of history. While you keep holding to your magic fairy tales, the world has evolved and religion is for stupid, weak, backwards people."

But the church continues doing what Noah did. Not shaking its fist at the world but faithfully going about doing the work of the Lord in obedience and patience.

By faith, by faith, by faith.

By faith we see what God has done in the past, what he is doing in the present, and what he will do in the future, when, after much delay from our perspective, the windows of heaven are opened in response (Gen. 7:11).

Once upon a time, the windows of the heavens opened and the rains came down for forty days and forty nights, enough rain to flood the earth. The flood brought death. But Noah and his family were saved.

Once upon a time, the windows of heaven opened and the Son of God came, and with him, a trail of glory and righteousness. And those who looked to him with the eyes of faith were saved from the wrath of God.

With the windows of heaven open, we see a vision of God as he truly is. He has parted the veil for us to peek into his glory. He is no one-dimensional deity. He is the majestic Triune God of the universe, arrayed in splendor and almighty in power. He is love and he is grace, and he is mercy and kindness. And he is holy and he is just and he is sovereign and he is wrath. When the windows of heaven opened in Noah's day, we see a bigger vision of who God is than we get in our feeble imaginations or in the popular conceptions of the religious media. We receive a stunning, terrifying vision of God's righteous judgment.

God is the holy and just judge of all creation, and he has the right *as God* to do with his creation as he wishes. But he is not an impulsive, vindictive God like the gods of the myths. He is not bloodthirsty. He is patient and longsuffering, the Bible tells us. But he will not put up with unrepentant sin forever. He saw that the world was wicked, that they only thought of evil continually: "And God said to Noah, 'I have determined to make an end of all flesh, for the earth is filled with violence through them. Behold, I will destroy them with the earth'" (Gen. 6:13). The very earth they enjoy and exploit, the ground that is cursed because of man's wickedness, will be instrumental in exacting the curse upon them.

Sin is such an offense to God that he could not be God if he didn't respond to it. His holiness is too great to turn a blind eye to wickedness. And though God later promises not to destroy the earth with a flood again, we still receive a picture of the latter judgment, the day of the ultimate destruction of the wicked:

> For as were the days of Noah, so will be the coming of the Son of Man. For as in those days before the flood they were eating and drinking, marrying and giving in marriage, until the day when Noah entered the ark, and they were unaware until the flood came and swept them all away, so will be the coming of the Son of Man. (Matt. 24:37–39)

Another flood is coming. One day the Lord will return finally, and the sinners who have rejected Christ will be destroyed, condemned to die eternally in the anguish of hell, while the sinners who have looked to Christ in faith will be saved.

The idea of hell is certainly out of fashion today. Modern sensibilities don't like it. We think we've outgrown it. But then something like 9/11 happens, something like Newtown happens. And then even atheists think evil needs to be dealt with. Even the staunchest of moral relativists believes there are some things that are wrong, and that when people do these wrong things, there should be consequences.

It often takes something like a terrorist attack or a child abuse scandal to wake us up to the reality of evil in our own neighbor-hoods. Some try to spin, to explain, to theorize the gravity of wick-edness away, but it proves too much.

The young man who murdered his mother and then twenty-six people at the school might have been autistic. He might have had social problems. He might have struggled with depression. But we should have no problem labeling what he did as evil.

What he did was wicked. It was the work of the Devil. Adam Lanza might not have been demon possessed, but what he did was satanic.

You can create a whole bunch of laws, but you won't fix this problem. The fundamental problem is spiritual.

But as soon as you bring up the spiritual aspect of this evil, the question arises: "Where was God?"

I'll tell you. God was in each room, by each victim. And he was in heaven, on his throne, righteously storing up wrath for this killer.

"It is appointed for man to die once, and after that comes judg-ment" (Heb. 9:27). We have reasonable evidence to believe that once Adam Lanza took his own life, avoiding the justice of earth, God was waiting for him with the justice that can't be avoided.

The unrepentant works of wickedness will receive the eternal condemnation of hell. This is eternal justice. It exists because evil is real.

This is the sobering truth about evil and the story God is telling about it: one day the holy and righteous Lord will flood the earth again—not with water, but with glory—and evil will be wiped out. Promised in God's Genesis 3 pronouncement and ratified in Christ's cross and resurrection, evil's days are numbered.

But the good news is this: as in Noah's day, the flood of glory that condemns the unrepentant will simultaneously lift the righteous.

God has always told his story this way. When he announces judgment, he also announces the way of escape. When he reveals condemnation, he promises consecration. When the curse of the law is declared, the cure of the gospel is not far behind. Look at 2 Peter 2:4–9:

> For if God did not spare angels when they sinned, but cast them into hell and committed them to chains of gloomy darkness to be kept until the judgment; if he did not spare the ancient world, but preserved Noah, a herald of righteousness, with seven others, when he brought a flood upon the world of the ungodly; if by turning the cities of Sodom and Gomorrah to ashes he condemned them to extinction, making them an example of what is going to happen to the ungodly; and if he rescued righteous Lot, greatly distressed by the sensual conduct of the wicked (for as that righteous man lived among them day after day, he was tormenting his righteous soul over their lawless deeds that he saw and heard); then the Lord knows how to rescue the godly from trials, and to keep the unrighteous under punishment until the day of judgment.

All the while God is reserving the unrighteous for punishment, he is rescuing the godly. The flood comes to destroy; Noah and his family are safe. The fire and brimstone comes to destroy Sodom; Lot is rescued. And when the great day of judgment finally comes, when the Devil and his angels and all who have believed their lies are sent to eternal fire, those who have trusted in Christ will be kept for everlasting glory.

In this way, then, it's important to see our place in the story. See, Noah's story, while real and historical, is also a foreshadow of the gospel of Christ Jesus. He is a type of Jesus. So while it's fine to view Noah as an example for us to be faithful and diligent and patient and trusting, we have to see our real place in the story of the flood not as faithful Noah but as faithful Noah's family.

Jesus, to quote Tim Keller, is the "true and better Noah."[1] Jesus is the Noah who builds a kingdom in his righteous obedience to

---

[1] Tim Keller, "What Is Gospel-Centered Ministry?" message delivered at the Gospel Coalition Conference (Chicago, May 23, 2007), http://resources.thegospelcoalition.org/library/what-is-gospel-centered-ministry-en/.

God that his bride may enter in and be saved. The righteousness of God established perfectly on the earth by Christ is an open door for all God's children, with rooms aplenty for all who belong to him. We would even suggest that since the gospel of Jesus announces the restoration of creation—that Christ is making all things new for the new heavens and new earth—the animals on the ark are a picture of that as well.

In any event, we see our place in the story as those saved by virtue of Christ's virtue just as those saved in Noah's day were saved by virtue of Noah's virtue. And the ark becomes a picture of the very intersection of judgment and grace itself: the cross.

The window of heaven opens up and in showing us a vision of God's glory in judgment and God's glory in grace, we see God's glory culminating in the cross of Jesus Christ.

At the cross, God's wrath is poured out—and also his love. Jesus absorbs the condemnation we deserve on the cross in a great act of love for God and for God's children. So that all who take Christ's cross will be spared their own.

Just as the ark becomes the means of escape from wrath, the cross becomes the means of escape from wrath. Just as Noah's family was saved by running to the ark, finding shelter in its wood constructed in Noah's obedience, God's children are saved by running to the cross, finding shelter in its blood-stained wood, the culmination of Christ's perfect obedience.

> By faith Noah, being warned by God concerning events as yet unseen, in reverent fear constructed an ark for the saving of his household. By this he condemned the world and became an heir of the righteousness that comes by faith. (Heb. 11:7)

The cross where Jesus died for the world still condemns the world that rejects it. And here's why: If you reject Christ's cross, where he took the punishment for sins, you reject his substitution for you and accept the punishment yourself.

All sin will be punished. Justice will be served.

The decision every person must make is this: Do I want to take my own punishment? Or do I want Jesus to take it for me?

Out of great love, God has sent his Son to die on the cross so that whoever believes in him will not perish but have everlasting life (John 3:16). There is no life anywhere else. Jesus says in John 14:6, "I am the way, and the truth, and the life. No one comes to the Father except through me." To reject Jesus is to reject life itself! Life *him*self.

When we open up the Word of God, the window of heaven opens to us. God wrote this, so it's his voice coming through. The vision we get in the Scriptures is not of some flat truth. God's no one-trick pony. He is glorious: his attributes are above us and eternal. He is higher than us, his ways are outside our comprehension. But he has made himself known in Christ Jesus, who is calling to us from his cross and empty tomb: Come! Find life here! Find rest here! Find satisfaction here! Find hope here! Find eternal joy here!

Don't go about just minding your own business, wasting day after day, oblivious to the coming judgment.

But what about the evil done *to* us? Can God make any sense of it?

I think of Joseph, receiving his brothers after years of separation. They had mocked him, tricked him, sold him, left him for dead. Yet he looks at this sorry lot of family-turned-enemies and he forgives them. He says something extraordinary to them: "You meant evil against me, but God meant it for good" (Gen. 50:20).

Remember that God's endgame is glory, so even evil is being used by God for his own sovereign purposes. I know that is a hard truth to consider; it is not easy to wrap our minds around and it opens up more questions than we had before we considered it. But think about it this way: Isn't it somehow more comforting to know that God has a purpose for evil, that he is meaning it somehow for his own glory and for the good of his children, than if he had no purpose for it?

If evil really were a rampant force, unrestrainable, uncontainable and completely rogue in the world and God had no plan or purpose for it, would that be *more* comforting? I would rather be confounded by the idea that God means something by allowing evil than be comfortable with the easy compartmentalization. The first idea is confusing but it is more comforting in the long run. The second idea is more intellectually comfortable but in the long run more hopeless and anxiety inducing.

The cross bends evil into submission; it gives evil a meaning it never intended on its own. So your cries for justice have been heard. Your vindication is coming. Evil may seem to triumph, but God's crosshairs are on it. Evil's days are numbered. And the Lord of vengeance is coming quickly.

Do you remember from chapter 2 that vision John has about Jesus making all things new? The new heavens and new earth are coming, and God is set to wipe away every tear and right every wrong. But lest we think this is some kind of all-excusing approval of sin itself, we see that the coming new world has severe implications for those who do not fear God. In the same vision, John quotes Jesus saying, "But as for the cowardly, the faithless, the detestable, as for murderers, the sexually immoral, sorcerers, idolaters, and all liars, their portion will be in the lake that burns with fire and sulfur, which is the second death" (Rev. 21:8).

When Christ returns, all we made wrong will be set right. The promise embedded in the curse of Genesis 3 is made explicit in the new covenant Scriptures where the Son of God first comes to live sinlessly, die sacrificially, and rise from the dead gloriously in order to redeem the sinners God loves. And while this Serpent is on a short leash now, in the end, when Christ returns, he will get lower than low:

> And he seized the dragon, that ancient serpent, who is the devil and Satan, and bound him for a thousand years. . . . And the devil who had deceived them was thrown into the lake of fire and sulfur where the beast and the false prophet were, and they will be tormented day and night forever and ever. (Rev. 20:2, 10)

Evil will be conquered, sin will be vanquished, death will vanish, and there will be justice for all.

The question is: Do you want your justice to be taken by Christ at the cross or by yourself in the age to come?

The Arc of Justice

In a 1964 sermon preached at Wesleyan University in Middletown, Connecticut, Martin Luther King Jr. repeated a line from an old Unitarian minister: "The arc of the moral universe is long, but it bends toward justice." The line now adorns the MLK memorial in Washington, DC. The meaning of this justice is likely as malleable as the arc in question. But we find some wonderful context for his oft-repeated line in an article he wrote six years earlier:

> Evil may so shape events that Caesar will occupy a palace and Christ a cross, but that same Christ arose and split history into A.D. and B.C., so that even the life of Caesar must be dated by his name. Yes, "the arc of the moral universe is long, but it bends toward justice." There is something in the universe which justifies William Cullen Bryant in saying, "Truth crushed to earth will rise again."[2]

That "something in the universe" is the Holy Spirit of God doing the will of the Father in glorifying the Son. The arc of the moral universe is bent because of the fall. But it's not off course. It is bent back into place at Christ's cross, where he has "disarmed the rulers and authorities and put them to open shame, by triumphing over them" (Col. 2:15), and it runs on toward his return, when "he delivers the kingdom to God the Father after destroying every rule and every authority and power" (1 Cor. 15:24).

That's the story God is telling about evil.

So how do we tell it? Primarily by preaching and sharing the gospel. But also by, as the Bible says, "doing justice" (Mic. 6:8).

After the flood of Noah's day has receded, we know that sin still

---

[2] Martin Luther King Jr., "Out of the Long Night," *The Gospel Messenger* (February 8, 1958), 3.

exists because God uses the mass condemnation of the wicked as a precedent for the ongoing work of justice.

God has stewarded us institutional means of administering justice in the world. When the Law comes, it's all very codified and specific, and even in the New Testament Paul says it is through God's granting that the government does not wield the sword in vain (Rom. 13:4). But we see the beginning groundwork for the justice system in Genesis 9:5–6:

> And for your lifeblood I will require a reckoning: from every beast I will require it and from man. From his fellow man I will require a reckoning for the life of man.
>
> "Whoever sheds the blood of man,
>   by man shall his blood be shed,
>   for God made man in his own image."

This is not a sanctioning of personal revenge or human wrath, but an instituting of governmental justice. Life is so precious, God is saying, and he is so holy, that the taking of life by another must be reckoned for by the taking of the murderer's life.

This justice satisfies but it can't ultimately bring peace. We see that it can't bring lasting peace in a few ways, mainly because we seem to have no shortage of crime despite the punishment. The law dissuades some potential criminals but certainly not enough. The laws work toward enacting justice when crimes are committed, but they don't do a complete job in preventing the existence of crime.

But, then, even when justice is enacted, we see again and again how imperfect this justice is, and, in some cases, how unjust this so-called justice is.

God here is instituting a foundation for capital punishment, but when the law specifies how and when this punishment ought to be carried out, its requirements are very thorough, and the evidence demanded very high and specific. According to God's law, you could not execute someone based on one eyewitness. You needed multiple witnesses. The burden of proof was heavy precisely because the taking of life, even of an alleged murderer's life, was seen as a terrible consequence. Because people are made in the image of God.

So in today's society, where we discover through DNA testing that we've locked up innocent people and have even executed innocent people, we see that our efforts at following God's mandate for justice are corrupt, tainted by our own zeal for the very justice we fail to achieve, tainted by corruption of the legal system, tainted by lies, and tainted by human frailty and imperfections.

But even when we get such justice right, it still doesn't bring the kind of peace we think it will.

Certainly for many families of murder victims, the execution of their loved one's murderer brings a kind of closure, a type of satisfaction that justice has been done, but it cannot bring back their loved one. It cannot bring real peace. It cannot bring real restoration of what was lost, only a sense of vindication in punishment. And many families have found the execution of the killer of their loved ones difficult.

Bruce and Janice Grieshaber are a New York couple whose daughter Jenna was murdered in her Albany apartment, six weeks before her nursing school graduation, by a guy who'd been released from prison early. Out of their grief, the Greishabers sought avenues of justice, and one of those was the popularization of a bill introduced in the state of New York to end parole for first-time violent felons, mandate that felons serve six-sevenths of their terms, and impose supervision on the felons after their release.

Prisoner rights activists slammed the bill as taking political advantage of rising crime. The Greishabers were not seen as bleeding-heart liberals in their campaigning for this law. But Janice has said, "I'm here to tell you, as the Mother of a homicide victim, that *the death penalty brings as much pain as it does relief, that it creates an entirely new layer of pain.*"[3]

Miriam Thimm Kelle, whose brother, Jim, was tortured to death, said:

---

[3] "Quotes by Families of Homicide Victims," Equal Justice USA online, http://ejusa.org/learn/quotes/victims.

Little did me and my family know then that when my brother's murderer was sentenced to death, we were sentenced too. Our sentence has been going on for 20 years and there has been no execution. For 20 years it has been all about Jim's killer. He is all my family and I ever hear about. Jim is never mentioned. . . . Having seen what the death penalty has done to my family, I have since changed my mind and now think it should be abolished.[4]

Kathy Garcia, whose aunt was murdered, says she used to support the death penalty until her family had to actually go through the process of seeking justice. She said, "The capital punishment system may have been put in place to serve us survivors, but it actually has been a colossal failure."[5]

Family after family who say they *do* support capital punishment say that even witnessing the execution of their loved one's murderer did not bring the closure they thought it would.

The point is not to be for or against the death penalty per se. (I think, personally, we have biblical grounds for it, but I also think the way we sometimes carry it out is far removed from the biblical burden of proof.) The point is to understand that the human administration of justice will always be tainted by imperfections, mistakes, wrong motivations, and sin. There is much injustice in our justice system.

We can't even get our moral sensibility right!

But the arc of our bent moral sensibilities is bent toward true and final and lasting justice.

Remember the secret to the universe.

Where do we find the lasting peace of true justice? In God's grace.

After the ark came the arc:

"Behold, I establish my covenant with you and your offspring after you," . . . And God said, "This is the sign of the covenant

---

[4] Ibid.
[5] Ibid.

that I make between me and you and every living creature that is with you, for all future generations: I have set my bow in the cloud, and it shall be a sign of the covenant between me and the earth." (Gen. 9:9, 12–13)

The rainbow now designated the sign of God's promise not to visit wrath on the earth by way of a flood again. But larger than that, the rainbow is another sign of God's promise to remove his wrath from his children.

The Hebrew word for *bow* in this text is the same Hebrew word used for the kind of bow one uses in battle, as in "bow and arrows." What God is talking about is laying down his weapons.

In his commentary on Genesis, Marcus Dods writes:

They accepted it as a sign that God has no pleasure in destruction, that He does not give way to moods, that He does not always chide, that if weeping may endure for a night joy is sure to follow. If any one is under a cloud, leading a joyless, hopeless, heartless life, if any one has much apparent reason to suppose that God has given him up to catastrophe, and lets things run as they may, there is some satisfaction in reading this natural emblem and recognising that without the cloud, nay, without the cloud breaking into heavy sweeping rains, there cannot be the bow, and that no cloud of God's sending is permanent, but will one day give place to unclouded joy.[6]

We keep seeking peace, peace, where there is no peace, and we only find our true lasting eternal joy-saturated peace when it comes by the Spirit of God straight from Father God in the gospel of the Son of God. It is in Christ Jesus's work that we see that God "lays down his bow."

And we can keep seeking peace even in God's good gifts—work, family, recreation, food, art and culture, the great outdoors—but we can't find the peace that endures forever until we find it in the

---

[6] Marcus Dods, *The Book of Genesis*, The Expositor's Bible (New York: A. C. Armstrong and Son, 1899), 74.

gospel. Because justice, while ordained by God, when administered by man can never truly satisfy.

But the covenant of grace is administered by God himself. So when we seek peace there, we truly find it. It's not tainted by sin because God is holy and his Son is sinless.

Until we find peace in the gospel, we find only the search for peace and therefore no peace at all. In Isaiah 57:21 we read, "There is no peace . . . for the wicked."

But to those who've put on Christ's righteousness, who've gotten into the ark of the cross, Isaiah 26:3 says: "You keep him in perfect peace whose mind is stayed on you, because he trusts in you."

The rainbow, then, is a sign of God's promise that he has hung up his bow, and it's a reminder to himself of his grace toward the earth. In the same way, the cross is a sign of God's promise that he has hung his Son up to die, and it's a reminder of his grace toward you that because Christ has taken the wrath, *the wrath is taken.*

At the cross of Christ, the wrath of God owed to sinners is absorbed, satisfied, and set aside for all eternity. Dead and done with. His anger is gone; his love remains and it endures. The lovingkindness of our Lord is everlasting. The steadfast love of the Lord never ceases. His mercies are new every morning.

Every day you mess up—and even when you're fessing up, you're messing up—but God's love is constant, always forgiving, always covering, always sustaining, always sourcing real peace deep inside.

Because Christ has come to take the condemnation, he takes it away into the wilderness and casts it into the void, and his precious blood is given as a covering for you. It speaks a better word than the blood of Abel, because while Abel's blood cried out for the justice we keep seeking, Jesus's blood cries out that justice has been accomplished, and every sin of yours—past, present, and future—has been accounted for and paid for. Now that the gospel takes dominion in your heart, it bears fruit and multiplies from one degree of glory to another, in mercy after mercy, precisely because we have received

Christ himself. As John 1:16 says, from his fullness we all received "grace upon grace."

In heaven, there is perfect peace. And when you trust in Christ, you join the Hero's side of the story, and heaven enters into you, indwells you, and gives you the heavenly peace inside—while you wait for the outside world to catch up with your inside.

Don't be on the wrong side of this story.

7

No More Tears

God's Plan for Pain

I don't particularly enjoy preaching funeral services, but I have had the great privilege of losing track of how many I've preached over the last six years. I preach as many as I can, because there is almost no other situation where unbelievers may be gathered at a time when they are uncharacteristically focused on matters of life or death, and the opportunity for gospel ministry is great. But even if the gospel doesn't resonate, identifying the problem the gospel addresses does. Funerals remind everybody that this world is not as it should be. People sitting in uncomfortable pews grappling with the disruption of death understand that, even if just for those brief moments.

A couple of years ago I conducted the memorial service for the son of a dear lady in our church. He had been in and out of prison, mostly for drug offenses, and his addictions had finally caught up with him. He died from an overdose of heroin.

I was at the building when the police were taping off the scene. And I was at the hospital with his mother while she waited to identify his body. And I looked straight into the eyes of his numerous friends on the morning of his funeral, pleading with them to repent of their addictions and seek forgiveness and satisfaction in Jesus Christ. An incredible pain had built up in the hearts and minds of this man's loved ones. Nearly all of his friends had troubles with drugs and crime themselves, so the church was a mixed bunch of his personal mourners and church folks there to support his mom. But everybody on that morning felt the same thing—we are broken.

To be human is to be broken. I didn't preach my best sermon that morning, but you could have heard a pin drop. I had decided to restate what we all know but try to medicate against, some with narcotics and others with money or family or fun or religion: We're all going to die. Life can be very painful. And then we die. When you cut to that chase in the middle of people's pain, you get their attention very quickly.

I remember one young man near the back of the church building. He was young, unkempt, and dressed in dingy blue jeans and a white T-shirt. I assumed he was one of the departed's friends, mainly because he was not dressed the way church folks typically dress for funerals. His gazed locked on my face like his life depended on it. His eyes became teary as I diagnosed the great essential sin of idolatry and held up the only true remedy of God's grace in Christ. I didn't know his story, but I bet I could come pretty close in guessing it. When the service was over, he immediately vanished.

I don't know if he placed his faith in Jesus or fled from his fear of death back into his deadly behaviors. Perhaps he reasoned that the pain of change was greater than the pain of staying the same. I don't know.

Sometimes the pain is so great we cannot imagine an escape from it and any suggested escapes seem too hard to believe. But we want to believe, don't we? We want to believe that pain is not forever.

The Problem of Pain

The pain begins as soon as the world breaks. After Adam and Eve disobey, the world fractures. And so must they:

To the woman he said,

"I will surely multiply your pain in childbearing;
    in pain you shall bring forth children.
Your desire shall be for your husband,
    and he shall rule over you."

And to Adam he said,

"Because you have listened to the voice of your wife
    and have eaten of the tree
of which I commanded you,
    'You shall not eat of it,'
cursed is the ground because of you;
    in pain you shall eat of it all the days of your life."
        (Gen. 3:16–17)

There is the beginning of the hurt. But the first couple had at least the benefit of God himself explaining to them where the pain was coming from and why it was coming. For millions of human beings after them, this knowledge has been suppressed (Rom. 1:18), and so pain always seems like a strange, foreign thing, an interloper into the world that ought to be "normal," which we assume to mean "pain free." But pain brings the need for the gospel right to the surface. When we hurt, our feelings of disconnection and insignificance are pronounced. We feel alone, hyperaware of our own suffering. And, especially if pain persists, we begin to wonder if there is any hope for us, if anyone cares about us, if there can be any escape from the suffering for miserable people like us.

This is why suffering pain apart from the promise of the gospel can be the height of misery. In our pain, we understand that the world is broken, that it's not as it should be, but we sense despair, because we don't know how—or even if!—it can be made right. If peace will ever come.

This feeling of despair is well considered by our friend Koheleth in that strange book Ecclesiastes. In all his wisdom, he senses a strange advantage in pain. He even says that feeling pain is better than not! This is what he writes in Ecclesiastes 7:2–3:

> It is better to go to the house of mourning
> than to go to the house of feasting,
> for this is the end of all mankind,
> and the living will lay it to heart.
> Sorrow is better than laughter,
> for by sadness of face the heart is made glad.

One thing you need to know about the man who wrote these words—most believe Koheleth is King Solomon—is that he had tried everything, done everything, and experienced everything. In Ecclesiastes 1–6, he surveys all he's achieved, all he's enjoyed, beginning with the fact that he was king of Israel. "I was king," he says. "And I acquired untold wisdom." In chapter 2, he says, "I sought all the pleasure I could." He built huge mansions that he adorned with beautiful gardens. Then with all his money and power he assembled the best entertainers and artists to perform for him. He ate the best foods in the world and drank the finest wines. He sought more and more money, more and more pleasure, and more and more women. He had accumulated and indulged in everything anyone can think of to make life worth living. Anything you can come up with to define what happiness is in this life, he had done it. And do you know what his conclusion about all of it is? Over and over he says, "It's all meaningless." He says, "It was like chasing the wind."

And so this man who says, "It's better to go to the house of mourning than to the house of feasting" and, "Sorrow is better than laughter" is not someone who doesn't know the difference. He knows what he's talking about. So we need to pay attention.

Why is he basically saying it's better to be at a funeral, to experience pain, than it is to be at a party, to be feeling fine? In what way is sorrow better than laughter?

Well, first, I think it's because the "house of mourning" makes us face the big questions we tend to avoid. Pain has a very *focusing* effect.

One thing Koheleth talks quite a bit about in Ecclesiastes is youth and aging. He's getting older. And he's starting to realize that all these things he's poured himself into to make life more enjoyable and more thrilling—to make himself happier—are really all serving as ways to avoid the fact that he's going to die. That he's getting older. That he's made from dust and that one day his body will be dust again.

And he's not even guaranteed a long life. Even if you could fill a hundred years with every pleasure imaginable, no one can ward off death, but so many people don't even get sixty years, or fifty, or forty, or thirty. Or ten.

The reality pain makes us face is this: We are going to die. You and I are going to die.

And we are not guaranteed a long life. Isn't kids getting cancer proof of that? Isn't young men having heart attacks proof of that?

So we have to face the big questions; we can't ward them off forever. Pain gets our attention on things that matter in a way that painlessness definitely does not. That is at least one of its benefits, an embedded mercy in the pain we were cursed with at the fall.

If we did not feel pain, we would not know the very important truth that we are needful of help, rescue, and redemption.

The Purpose of Pain

In August 2014, a judge in England ruled that a woman could order the euthanization of her twelve-year-old daughter who had suffered from a series of medical conditions leaving her severely disabled. The little girl was not on life support and her condition was not fatal. But her mother argued that her daughter had no quality of life. The judge agreed, setting for the first time a precedent for the taking of adolescent life due to disability, and all her nutrition and medicine were removed. Later, the mom said this: "I miss my beautiful girl every day and although I know it was the right thing to do, I will never forgive myself."[1]

Isn't that an interesting thing to say? The cognitive dissonance is staggering. "It was the right thing to do. But I can never forgive myself."

We should not be glib or dismissive of this mother's real concerns about the pain of her daughter and the depth of despair she felt, helpless to reverse it. But decisions like these speak to a fatal misunderstanding of what is really happening behind the scenes in creation. The word that keeps coming up in these situations is *dignity*. Proponents of physician-assisted suicide and the like are constantly speaking to the dignity of the person suffering.

On November 1, 2014, a young woman named Brittany Maynard took her own life to avoid the painful progressive death of cancer. Maynard was diagnosed with glioblastoma, a brain tumor, earlier that year and given six months to live. In going public with her decision to take her life into her own hands, she asserted that it was her right to "die with dignity." Maynard wrote:

> I've had the medication for weeks. I am not suicidal. If I were, I would have consumed that medication long ago. I do not want to die. But I am dying. And I want to die on my own terms.
>
> I would not tell anyone else that he or she should choose death with dignity. My question is: Who has the right to tell me that I don't deserve this choice? That I deserve to suffer for weeks or months in tremendous amounts of physical and emotional pain?[2]

Again, these are real issues with real philosophical and emotional depth that should not be glossed over. But the fundamental

---

[1] Paisley Gilmour, "Why I Begged Judge to End My Sick Daughter's Life: 'Nancy Is No Longer My Girl, She's a Shell,'" *Mirror* online, October 25, 2014, http://www.mirror.co.uk/news/real-life-stories/begged-judge-end-sick-daughters-4509235/.

[2] Brittany Maynard, "My Right to Die with Dignity at 29," *CNN* online, November 2, 2014, http://www.cnn.com/2014/10/07/opinion/maynard-assisted-suicide-cancer-dignity/

assertion in nearly all these cases—that to suffer is undignified—is only true if suffering has no meaning, no purpose, no part in a bigger plan that could give earthly suffering, even long-time suffering, a resonance that actually makes it worth it.

I lost two friends to brain tumors in 2013. They weren't just people I knew; they were friends. Anne was in her early sixties. Her brain tumor was found too late, and it was too aggressive for the surgeries she had and the treatment she received to prevent her dying a few months after diagnosis. Richard was in his early thirties. He fought his cancer for a few years, but eventually succumbed, leaving behind a young wife and two children under the age of six.

I watched their declining states up close and personally. I watched their spouses feed them, clean them, carry them around. We read to them, sang to them, prayed with them, and cried with them. I watched as Anne quickly became more and more babylike, conscious but unable to understand or respond. I watched Richard decline into a state of constant sedation. I watched them both waste away and die.

The decisions that their families had to make in those final stages are not to be envied. And countless people make them every day, seeking to do the right thing while balancing the desire to keep their loved ones with them with the desire to mercifully liberate them from their pain and suffering. As I write this, I have another close friend, Natalie, who is slowly dying of pancreatic cancer. She was diagnosed shortly after Easter 2014. By the time you read this, she will likely have passed. As often as I can, I go to sit with her and read the Bible and reminisce about church life. Natalie has decided not to seek any treatment for her cancer. She is not taking her own life, but rather allowing the cancer to do what it appears God has allowed it to do. Maybe you don't see the difference between the two. But there's one thing I cannot deny after watching these three friends, and several more besides, suffer well—there has been nothing undignified about any of it. It is not neat or tidy or simple or painless. But there's no denying the dignity.

I propose that you cannot really see that dignity unless you see the larger story God is telling. If you have the narrative of God's glory and his modus operandi of grace in mind, any pain becomes a little more understandable—*worth it*, even—because you realize that this world, and thus this pain, is not all that there is. And there lies another of the ways "the house of mourning" is better than the house of feasting. Pain gets our attention, and it helps sensitize us to the truth. Or, at least, it ought to.

C. S. Lewis once said that "pain is God's megaphone."[3] He uses pain not only to affirm our hunch that the world is not as it should be, but also to proclaim our need for him. We would not sense a need for God if we did not feel any kind of pain.

Being in pain doesn't just make us hear the big questions; being in pain helps us be more open to the truth of the gospel. It prepares us to hear the answers to our questions.

See, in the story God is telling with the world, getting hurt and even dying are not the worst things that can happen to you. As much effort as we put into getting healthy and forestalling death—through exercise and eating right and benefiting from medical advances—we mistakenly think that dying is the worst fate that could befall us. But it's not.

In Matthew 10:28 Jesus says, "And do not fear those who kill the body but cannot kill the soul." In other words, Jesus is saying, "Look, all that person can do is kill you. That's it." "Rather," he says in the same verse, "fear him who can destroy both soul and body in hell." Who's he talking about? Who can destroy both body *and* soul in hell? He's talking about God; he's talking about himself.

In other words, Jesus is saying, "Dying isn't the worst thing that can happen to you. Dying *after* you die is the worst thing that can happen to you."

For Jesus, missing out on eternal life with him in the painless, griefless everlasting joy of heaven—and the new heavens and earth to come—is the worst thing that can happen to you. Trading eternal

---

[3] C. S. Lewis, *The Problem of Pain* (New York: HarperCollins, 1996), 91.

joy for temporary happiness is the worst decision you can make. The only security any of us can have is found in Jesus. To not believe in the good news of Jesus's work, then, is to agree to eternal condemnation after you die. It is to move from the pain of this life into the eternal, agonizing pain of the next.

Oh, but we think we know the way to dignify pain and suffering! If we can't avoid it, we can turn it into inspirational stories. We can medicate it with drugs and self-help and sentimentality and New Age spirituality. All of these things are grasps at connection and significance. When in pain, we are hyperaware of our own selves, and in response we dive further into self, seeking meaning "somewhere within."

But if we can't keep the pain away, if we can't avoid death, what makes us think the answer to connection and significance is found inside our painful, dying bodies? Pain tells us we are broken, and we think we can heal ourselves?

It's all one big self-justification project, a way we make the story of our pain ultimately a story about ourselves.

But there's no peace or security in self-centeredness.

Thus, for as much as the pain in our bodies and in our hearts screams out for us to become focused on ourselves, the story God tells would have us tune our pain outside of ourselves, to see it as a static frequency in need of that signal from "outer space."

Pain should make us despair of ourselves. But it should not make us despair.

The Promise of Pain

Ultimately, pain should point us to the saving pain of Jesus. I think this is what Koheleth is getting at in Ecclesiastes 7:3 when he says, "By sadness of face the heart is made glad." He's saying that you can get to temporary happiness any old time—any medication will do, and that's what all these attempts to make ourselves happy apart from Jesus end up being: drugs to medicate us from sadness and the inevitability of death. But you can't get to lasting, deep, abiding, eternal joy except through finding out the only answer to death.

The only antidote to pain, to death itself, is found in the painful death of Jesus Christ.

One of my favorite moments from the life of Jesus in the Gospels is when he attends the funeral of his friend Lazarus. It's the passage that includes the shortest verse in the entire Bible: "Jesus wept" (John 11:35).

Jesus is at the grave of Lazarus, and he, along with Lazarus's sisters Mary and Martha, is grieving the loss, when Martha says to him, "Jesus, if you'd only been here four days ago, you could have healed my brother. Lazarus would not have died" (see John 11:21).

Martha doesn't remember that Jesus never shows up late. And if you're in a relationship with Jesus, he will never leave you in a place of total insecurity. Jesus responds to Martha: "I am the resurrection and the life. Whoever believes in me, though he die, yet shall he live, and everyone who lives and believes in me shall never die." Then he drives this provocative point home by pressing those in the house of mourning to respond to his claim to be the be-all and end-all, the only source of real life in existence, the only antidote to death, the only Rescuer and Redeemer and Reverser of the curse of death. He says to Martha, "Do you believe this?"

And to prove his point, to prove that belief in him is the only way to cheat death, Jesus goes to the mouth of Lazarus's tomb and shouts, "Lazarus, come forth!"

And Lazarus rises from the dead.

It is a great foreshadow of Jesus's own resurrection from the dead, and it is a great foreshadow of what the Bible promises to those who die trusting Jesus: They will be raised again on the day of judgment and given new bodies—bodies that don't get hurt, bodies that don't mourn, bodies that don't die.

Pain might number your days, but because Jesus Christ is the victor over sin and death, for those who know him, pain's days are numbered.

When you have trusted in Jesus, your outlook on death changes. The Bible says that believers in Jesus grieve as those with hope (1 Thess. 4:13).

This does not make pain painless, of course, but it doesn't make it purposeless either. Pain for those who trust Christ is not pointless. It is being stewarded toward something, drafted into a story of glory and wonder and eternal joy.

Genesis 16 tells us a story about the pain suffered as the result of injustice. God has made a covenant promise to Abram to make a mighty nation out of him, but in the previous chapter, Abram complains, essentially saying, "What are you going to give me, God? When are you going to do this? I don't have any kids. One of my servants is going to be my heir."

And God says, "No, I'm going to give you a son. A lot else, but also your very own son." Genesis 15:6 says that Abram believed God and this belief was credited to him as righteousness.

But we get a few years on and the son hasn't arrived yet. Sarai has not conceived, the doubt has built up again and the bitterness along with it, and Abram and Sarai do what they normally do when God seems to be taking too long—what we all do when it seems like God is taking too long. They try to take matters into their own hands.

"God's working is slow," they figure. Maybe he can't be trusted. (Which is what we're saying when we do things our own way and in our own timing: "God can't be trusted.") So Sarai hatches a scheme and tells Abram to take their maid Hagar and conceive a child with her.

And so the very end of Genesis 16:2 is very important: "And Abram listened to the voice of Sarai."

He stopped listening to the promises of God, and he started listening to the doubting, distrustful instructions of his wife. The reversal here is very reminiscent of Adam and Eve in the garden, where the Serpent is tempting Eve, and Adam, apparently, is just standing there, not protecting his wife, not interceding for her, but passively observing, and he lets his wife take the lead into distrust and disobedience and then follows suit.

Abram doesn't need any help with sin and doubt. It's not like he's a blank slate whose flaws are all his wife's fault. He has led her into some awful situations. And oftentimes when a man is extremely passive in the way of godly leadership of his home or has exploited his role as head and done great sin to his wife, the wife may overcompensate as a defense mechanism, as a means of self-protection. Maybe that's what's happening here. Abram has put Sarai in some terrible situations, and he doesn't seem to be changing his ways, so she's figuring, "Look, if he's not going to be a reliable leader who cares about me, maybe I ought to come up with my own plan."

Neither one of them is trusting in God's promise.

So Abram takes Hagar. Do not let the plainspeak of the text fool you. This is a bad thing. Abram has exploited his authority over Hagar; he and Sarai both have done this. He is treating Hagar like something he owns. They didn't ask her permission.

It says in verse 3 that Sarai gives Abram Hagar as his wife. They are not just departing from God's design for marriage as one man and one woman, but they are treating Hagar not as a sacred image bearer of God—a person with thoughts and feelings who as a human being is made in the image of God—but as property.

This is not just sexual harassment. It is sexual injustice. And in those days not only did women not have much power unless a man gave it to them, but a servant had even less. No voice. So Hagar is being exploited and sinned against greatly.

Next to Abram handing off Sarai to Pharaoh to do God-knows-what with her, this is one of the earliest examples of sexual exploitation in the Bible.

And it doesn't turn out the way Abram and Sarai figured it would. According to verse 4, Hagar, after conceiving a child by Abram, begins to look with contempt on Sarai. What for? Is it a "Look, I've got a child and you don't" kind of smug contempt? A kind of comeuppance? Or is it a "I can't believe you'd do this to me?" kind of contempt? Maybe both. Hagar has been victimized, and maybe her own need for control and power to compensate for the injustice prompts her to "lord it over" Sarai.

In any event, Sarai gets sick of it. Abram gets sick of hearing about it, and the thing continues to be a big mess. If you're tracking the story, you see that weak, passive Abram has taken Hagar as a wife and conceived a child with her. And if that wasn't exploitation enough, he now treats her like a cast-off: "Whatever you want to do with her, Sarai, go ahead and do" (see Gen. 16:6). So Sarai, in effect, throws Hagar away. At the end of verse 6, she "deals harshly" with her, to the extent that Hagar takes off carrying her unborn child.

Not all pain is physical. Sometimes we'd prefer physical pain to the kind of inner trauma that can persist, haunt, damage. I've had emotionally and verbally abused wives say to me, "I almost wish my husband *had* hit me. It'd be easier to see, easier to explain, harder for someone to ignore."

What a terrible prospect, what a feeling of hopelessness and alienation, that somebody would wish for physical hurt because it would be easier to address, to manage, or to fix than the hidden emotional hurt.

Maybe right now you feel a bit like Hagar. Someone has hurt you, someone has done an injustice to you—and maybe he or she is continuing to do so. Maybe you don't know what to do about it.

Or maybe your hurt is somehow indiscernible. There's no clear explanation for it. You just know you hurt. Maybe the dark cloud of depression and anxiety hangs over you, and you can't figure out how to shake it. You feel alone, hopeless.

You need to know that God has not forgotten you. And he has not forsaken you.

In Genesis 16, the angel of the Lord finds Hagar out in the wilderness. She's alone, she's afraid, and she's feeling used and thrown away. And God comes near.

She needs to know what to do, where to go, and how to make

sense of this great wrong that's been done to her and the great pain that has resulted.

The Lord's messenger tells her to go back and submit to Sarai. Now, we should not take this as a blanket endorsement for the abused or victimized to submit themselves to more abuse and victimization. Please don't read it that way. Too much damage has been done in the evangelical church in instructing victimized people to keep themselves in harm's way.

But this specific instruction to this specific person does have a general application for all people everywhere, and it is this: "Trust me."

See, God doesn't send Hagar back into a difficult spot without compensation, without hope. He says, "Trust me. I'm writing a magnificent story here, the end of which you don't yet see, but I will provide the vindication and restoration you are longing for."

God says to Hagar, as he said to Abram, "I'm going to make a great people out of you too. You will be compensated for this; there will be justice. You are not forgotten, you are not thrown away by me."

Hear this, those of you who are hurting: God has not thrown you away. He has not forgotten you. He will plead your case. He will redeem the time you spend in pain.

Consider Psalm 126:5–6:

Those who sow in tears
    shall reap with shouts of joy!
He who goes out weeping,
    bearing the seed for sowing,
shall come home with shouts of joy,
    bringing his sheaves with him.

Consider Isaiah 61:2–3, which says that when the day of the Lord comes, God will come:

to comfort all who mourn;
to grant to those who mourn in Zion—

to give them a beautiful headdress instead of ashes,
the oil of gladness instead of mourning,
    the garment of praise instead of a faint spirit;
that they may be called oaks of righteousness,
    the planting of the LORD, that he may be glorified.

Consider Jesus beginning his sermon on the mount with these declarations:

Blessed are the poor in spirit, for theirs is the kingdom of heaven.
Blessed are those who mourn, for they shall be comforted.
Blessed are the meek, for they shall inherit the earth.
Blessed are those who hunger and thirst for righteousness, for they shall be satisfied. (Matt. 5:3–6)

You Christians who hurt and wait, hurt and wait, hurt and wait, *your day is coming.*

Habakkuk 2:3 says, "If it seems slow, wait for it; it will surely come; it will not delay."

So what does Hagar's day look like? God sends her back into difficulty but he makes a promise that he never makes to any other matriarch. Hagar is the only woman in the Bible to receive a promise such as the one in Genesis 16:10: "I will surely multiply your offspring so that they cannot be numbered for multitude."

An interesting, powerful dynamic immediately arises. See, Hagar does not return to a comfortable, welcoming environment. She and Sarai never get along, and even after Isaac is born, Hagar rubs Sarai the wrong way and both Hagar and Ishmael get thrown out again. But God comes along and looks after them. Because that's what he does. So imagine for Hagar, living in a hostile environment, it could be extraordinarily empowering to know "God's going to take care of me." It's extremely liberating.

When you believe God will handle it; when you believe your reward is in heaven; when you believe God will mete out justice in a satisfactory way; when you believe God can be trusted; when you believe it's all going to get set right in the by-and-by, you worry less, you stew less, you try to control things less, you seek revenge less.

You can endure great difficulty with confidence and joy when you believe God is looking after you. Paul says this about his constant pain: "For this light momentary affliction is preparing for us an eternal weight of glory beyond all comparison" (2 Cor. 4:17). How could he call his pain a "light momentary affliction"? This is a guy who's been tortured, shipwrecked, betrayed, and assaulted, and who spends most of his time in prisons and before hostile crowds who want to stone him. And on top of all that, he has a strange "thorn in the flesh" (2 Cor. 12:7). How can he call all this "light"? How can he call it "momentary"?

Well, he was comparing it to that "eternal weight of glory beyond all comparison."

Paul knew that God was telling a story about everything, and that this meant even his pain was being swept up into the grand narrative of God's redeeming work in Jesus Christ to restore the world and vanquish that pain forever.

When Jesus takes us into his life, he takes our pain too. Tim Keller writes:

> At the end of his life we come to the *Passion*, literally the sufferings of Jesus. He was abandoned, denied, and betrayed by all the people he had poured his life into, and on the cross he was forsaken even by his father (Matt 27:46). This final experience, ultimately unfathomable to us, means infinite, cosmic agony beyond the knowledge of any of us on earth . . . God the Son took the punishment we deserved, including being cut off from the Father. And so God took into his own self, his own heart, an infinite agony—out of love for us.[4]

Knowing this truth, Paul considers his hurts part of God's story. He sees them as contributing to the glory of Christ, and, conversely, he sees the glory of Christ contributing meaning to his

---

[4] Timothy Keller, *Walking with God through Pain and Suffering* (New York: Dutton, 2013), 150.

hurts (Col. 1:24). He considers it a privilege to suffer (Phil. 1:29), because it makes him more like Jesus (2 Cor. 4:10).

Seeing the pain that still lay ahead of her, Hagar did not seek dignity in a quick, painless death. She found her dignity in the promise of God: "So she called the name of the LORD who spoke to her, 'You are a God of seeing,' for she said, 'Truly here I have seen him who looks after me'" (Gen. 16:13).

This reminds me of one of my favorite passages from the book of Exodus:

> During those many days the king of Egypt died, and the people of Israel groaned because of their slavery and cried out for help. Their cry for rescue from slavery came up to God. And God heard their groaning, and God remembered his covenant with Abraham, with Isaac, and with Jacob. God saw the people of Israel—and God knew. (Ex. 2:23–25)

Do you feel like the pain is hopeless? Endless? Do you feel used up, thrown away, hurt, doubtful? Do you feel like running away from difficulties, or trapped and wishing you could?

God sees. God knows. And God is looking after you.

You can trust him. And if you do, your reward is sure and surely coming soon.

If you want to cheat death, you can do so only by trusting in the One who conquered death. His name is Jesus Christ. And he has come in the love of God the Father to die for the sins of the world and rise again to reverse the curse of death and purchase the gift of eternal life for all who would believe in him. So if you feel sorrow over your sins against God and sorrow over Christ's death for you, you are ripe for the kind of gladness that will never go away, the kind of gladness that will sustain you for all eternity, the kind of gladness that will resound and abound for infinite days long after this world and everyone in it has crumbled to dust. Don't miss out on the gladness of heart Koheleth talks about in Ecclesiastes 7:3 because you're too bored with or too scared of the sorrow of face it talks about. See Jesus on the cross and see that he has died for you—to forgive you, to redeem you, to restore you, to save you.

For those who trust in Christ, the pain is not wasted. The shadows this side of the grave give way to the great light beyond. In his story *The Great Divorce*, C. S. Lewis writes: "[Some mortals] say of some temporal suffering, 'No future bliss can make up for it,' not knowing that Heaven, once attained, will work backwards and turn even that agony into a glory."

The promise of the gospel shows us the end of the story God is telling with pain. For those who reject God's story, the pain will not end. It will get worse. They have to keep their pain for all eternity. But for those who trust in God's glorious end by trusting in Jesus, their pain once taken vicariously by Christ at the cross will be cast forever into the grave of separation, never to appear again.

Joni Eareckson Tada, who has lived in constant states of pain even as she's lived most of her life with crippling paralysis, has said this:

> You know, though, I always say that in a way, I hope I can take my wheelchair to heaven with me—I know that's not biblically correct, but if I were able, I would have my wheelchair up in heaven right next to me when God gives me my brand new, glorified body. And I will then turn to Jesus and say, "Lord, do you see that wheelchair right there? Well, you were right when you said that in this world we would have trouble, because that wheelchair was *a lot* of trouble! But Jesus the weaker I was in that thing, the harder I leaned on you. And the harder I leaned on *you*, the stronger I discovered you to be. So thank you for what you did in my life through that wheelchair. And now," I always say jokingly, "you can send that wheelchair to hell, if you want."[5]

We can do the same with our pain on that final day. And we will cry out in adorational ecstasy in that moment, like the great cry of

---

[5] Joni Eareckson Tada, "The Holiest of Wheelchairs," Joni and Friends online, May 25, 2010, http://www.joniandfriends.org/radio/5-minute/holiest-wheelchairs/.

the Moravian missionaries: "May the Lamb that was slain receive the reward of his suffering!"[6]

We will cast our sufferings finally on Christ, and he will in turn cast them into the void.

The apostle John sees the vision of the end of this story and the beginning of the next one, as he witnesses the great Christian multitude brought up out of the deep, troubling pains of life in a fallen world:

> Then one of the elders addressed me, saying, "Who are these, clothed in white robes, and from where have they come?" I said to him, "Sir, you know." And he said to me, "These are the ones coming out of the great tribulation. They have washed their robes and made them white in the blood of the Lamb.
>
> "Therefore they are before the throne of God,
> and serve him day and night in his temple;
> and he who sits on the throne will shelter them with his
> presence.
> They shall hunger no more, neither thirst anymore;
> the sun shall not strike them,
> nor any scorching heat.
> For the Lamb in the midst of the throne will be their
> shepherd,
> and he will guide them to springs of living water,
> and God will wipe away every tear from their eyes."
> (Rev. 7:13–17)

Every tear. Wiped away.

Amazing. Beautiful.

What is God doing with pain? He is calling out to you through it, that you would call out to him from it. And if you do, he promises to give it meaning, purpose, and *an expiration date*.

---

[6] Quoted in Patrick Johnstone, *The Future of the Global Church: History, Trends, and Possibilities* (Colorado Springs: Global Mapping International, 2011), 133. The cry of the Moravian missionaries was made famous by Paris Reidhead's famous sermon, "Ten Shekels and a Shirt" (1965), http://www.sermonaudio.com/sermoninfo.asp?SID=10180222445.

8

A Little R & R

God's Plan for Fun

It's Sunday afternoon. I was up at five in the morning going over my sermon. At the church gathering four hours later, I met with people, prayed, counseled, and of course preached. I take preaching very seriously. Preaching takes me very seriously too. I'm usually worn out mentally and emotionally, if not physically, when I'm finished, but there are more people to meet, more directions to give, more advice to offer. Finally I made it home. I feel like a shell of a man. I just want to plop down on the couch with a warm cup of coffee or an ice cold Coke Zero. From early September to early February there is a gift from heaven waiting for me on Sunday afternoon, something I find in that glowing idiot box in my living room that helps me in ways I cannot quite explain. This thing is called the NFL.

I know for many this makes no sense. Football is a violent game, and these days there are rapid-fire stats and flashy graphics that go along with watching it on television, but watching NFL football games (especially on a Sunday afternoon) is deeply restful for me. It's like comfort food for my eyes.

Sometimes I hear guys talking about baseball in these really strange ways. It takes on the quality of myth; it provokes some kind of Zen-like state for them. The game isn't just a game. Baseball isn't baseball. It's Americana. It's grandma's house and warm apple pie and peace on earth for a few hours in somebody's living room. Well, I don't understand that at all. I find baseball incredibly boring. It's okay to play, but frustratingly difficult to watch. But the way these guys feel about baseball, I feel about football. I find watching men play really hard really *restful.*

There's a conflation of God's good gifts there, an intersection of things that you wouldn't think should go together—hard play and good rest. I know guys, particularly in Vermont, who like to spend their days off from work *working.* Only, to them, it's not work. They get a Saturday or Sunday off from their regular jobs, the ones that help them put food on the table and heat in the house, and they spend those days chopping wood, building fences, plowing earth, and what-have-you. Or they cycle hundreds of miles or hike up hundreds of feet. None of that sounds restful to me; it's not how I want to spend my day off from work. But for these folks, it doesn't feel like work. I mean, it's hard, it's tough, it's sweaty, but it somehow relaxes them in ways their day jobs do not.

I used to feel that way about playing basketball and football on the weekends. I would sweat, get banged around, and be sore for a few days afterward, and I loved every second of it. I couldn't get enough. (This was in my younger days, when I was actually good at those things.)

How is it that recreation that takes a lot of effort and costs us blood, sweat, and tears can actually serve to help us relax in ways that a day job spent sitting in a chair all week can't? I do not have a physically strenuous job. Standing up forty minutes preaching into a microphone is probably the most physically taxing thing I do as a pastor. Most of my time is spent sitting down to visit with people or sitting down at my desk to study and write. So why does it wear me out? Why does it so often feel like work, while getting outside in the frigid cold with my girls, getting out of breath and bruised up as we spend hours sledding in the snow, feel fun? Restful?

God is such a beautiful storyteller. He's an expert artist. It is one of the great wonders of common grace that he can make boring jobs exhausting and exciting adventures relaxing. I think it may be a way that he facilitates the redemption of our impulse to self-justification. Our flesh likes the idea of effort. We especially by our sinful natures like the idea of justifying ourselves through our works. But when we try to earn salvation with our effort, we only find ourselves weary. So God in the cleverest of wisdom makes it so that we only truly feel refreshed when we pour our energies into resting.

And he really does want us to rest.

Take a Load Off

As we learned in chapter 5, work isn't bad. Work is not a consequence of the fall. God invented work, and he gave it to Adam and Eve before sin entered the world as the means of taking dominion. This is where our good "doctrine of vocation" comes from. But now we have to factor into our view of work the reality that after the fall, work is hard. "That's why they call it work," as my dad (and probably yours) used to say.

Now, according to the curse of sin, work comes by the sweat of the brow. It causes pain. But part of our doctrine of vocation must include right thinking about rest. Because even though work was not necessarily hard before the fall, the origins of rest do not come after the fall. Like work, rest began before sin made everything so difficult.

> Thus the heavens and the earth were finished, and all the host of them. And on the seventh day God finished his work that he had done, and he rested on the seventh day from all his work that he had done. So God blessed the seventh day and made it holy, because on it God rested from all his work that he had done in creation. (Gen. 2:1–3)

So rest is not merely a compensation for hard work. It goes deeper than that. We see in this passage that God himself rested. Why? It's not like he was tired. Speaking the wonders of the universe was no taxing effort for him.

Even after the fall, when God reaches back to creation history to include in his Ten Commandments the rule, "Remember the Sabbath day, to keep it holy," he is not meaning rest so much as a way to recuperate from the work week, even though it most definitely is that, but more as a way to remember God's creative purposes, to reflect on God's God-ness, in a way. This is why rest can look like lots of different things, including work to some people.

One of the things I've had to say about rest to my ministry context in Vermont, where that New England work ethic is still strong, is that rest isn't laziness. Rest isn't laziness, first of all, because laziness is a sin and God cannot sin, and there is God in Genesis 2:1–3 resting. Again, he's not tired. But he has stopped working. He stopped doing what he was doing for the majority of the week. We might better call resting *pausing*.

In any event, whatever is restful for you, even if it's strenuous activity, the command to rest presupposes you've been all along actually working. If you don't work, it's not rest you're engaging in but idleness. Koheleth says, "Sweet is the sleep of a laborer" (Eccles. 5:12).

We certainly do have a laziness problem in the United States, but we also have a workaholism problem. According to an article in the *Boston Globe*:

> A growing number of North American workers do not take all of their annual allotted days off, companies report. Although some of those days can be rolled over into the next year, workplace analysts estimate that more than half of employees lose at least some vacation every year.
>
> Working nonstop is a "subtle badge of honor" in today's world, said Matt Norquist, general manager at the global workplace consultancy Right Management in New York. Its survey

recently found that 70 percent of workers do not use all their vacation time.[1]

The article says that working nonstop is a subtle badge of honor. But God says it's not a badge of honor. Working nonstop is not honorable.

If God is not above rest, who do we think we are?

God is so interested in rest that he keeps commanding it right and left in the Old Testament. Every seventh year, the children of Israel were to let the land rest (Lev. 25:4). You're supposed to let your animals rest on the Sabbath too. How about this honeymoon law?

> When a man is newly married, he shall not go out with the army or be liable for any other public duty. He shall be free at home one year to be happy with his wife whom he has taken. (Deut. 24:5).

Clearly, God is interested in rest.

This is the crucial point for those who have trouble resting because "things have to be done." Because do you know what else has to be done? The commandments of God. And God says, "Sit down. Take a load off."

If you are working, resting is not laziness. It's not wrong, it's not shameful, it's not bad. It is good. And it is an order from the Most Holy God.

But he doesn't order you to rest just for kicks. He wants you to rest because he knows that rest is good for you. Now, we know all kinds of information about how medically and bodily helpful resting is. Workaholics run great risks of heart attacks and strokes. But Jesus gives us an interesting perspective on Sabbath rest in response to a critical challenge against his activity on the Sabbath.

As Jesus and his disciples picked grain to eat on the Sabbath,

---

[1] Katie Johnston, "For Majority of Workers, Vacation Days Go Unused," *Boston Globe* online, December 30, 2013, http://www.bostonglobe.com/business/2013/12/30/for-majority-workers -vacation-days-unused/7X1VwsRbVahLOzy98wnTyH/story.html/.

the religious leaders challenge him: "You're not supposed to work this day!"

And he said to them, "The Sabbath was made for man, not man for the Sabbath" (Mark 2:27).

God doesn't command rest for our frustration, but for our good. And the blessed, holy day of the Sabbath is not made so we'll just have one more rule to conform to. It's made *for* us. It's made for our benefit.

One thing Jesus is saying is that yes, you have to obey the Sabbath law, but the law is not there to be legalistic about. For some people, working on their car is restful. For some, running a marathon is restful. I don't understand that myself. But for others of us, playing sports is restful. You're expending energy but it's not work per se. Jesus is helping us see that rest doesn't have to mean sitting completely still (although often it does). The law isn't given to restrain us from all activity but to keep us from constantly working. And not all activity is work.

Jesus's words here also help us not to restrict the Sabbath but to *expand* it. From his teaching here to the laws in the Old Testament about various rest days and rest years and feast days and such, we are beginning to learn that Sabbath is less about a particular day and more about a particular rhythm. "Work six days, rest one" is a rhythm. Your Sabbath may be Saturday or Sunday or whenever your day off is. But the rhythm ought to carry on into the fabric of your life.

You who work regularly ought to rest regularly. You ought to carve out a couple of mini-Sabbaths during the day every day. You ought to regularly take an extended Sabbath—take your vacation days, take a sabbatical, take a drive, or take a nap.

None of God's laws are given so that we would be legalistic about them, and this includes the command to rest. Sabbath rest is given for our good.

And here is where we open the door to the great heavenly rumpus room. God is not a miser with joy, so while our rest ought to regularly look like sleeping or simply sitting in prayerful silence, it should also come with great bounding leaps of fun.

Play Hard

We are not meant to be "perpetually solemn," according to C. S. Lewis. "We must play."[2]

This is something children understand instinctively. They don't even have to be reminded to play. They just do. Part of growing up is realizing that there are times you shouldn't be playing, of course, but part of growing up ought to be remembering that there are times we should!

The spirit of play is part of the creativity of rest. Little kids get out of breath. They get flushed cheeks. They come falling into the door at dinnertime after a long afternoon playing in the neighborhood smelling like little puppy dogs. They have skinned knees and grime under their fingernails. There are rocks in their pockets and grass stains on their sleeves. Their hair is messy and their eyes are wide. It's hard work playing so well. They cannot wait to get back outside and do it all again. This is all so God-glorifyingly beautiful.

The average eight-year-old boy on your block is a little Michelangelo of play. Take his toys away, and he will make a tower with the cushions, a battleship with a cardboard box. He will have at you with a wrapping paper tube. (And his little sister throws the most delightful tea parties for invisible royalty the likes of which no fairy tale could ever imagine.)

Why is playing hard so important? Because in our play we create and imagine and therefore tap into the very creative heart of God. We echo his story with our narratives of play. This is why on the playground little boys are playing cops and robbers or doing battle and little girls are playing house. They are vanquishing evil, subduing the earth, building civilization. And because all of this effort reflects the heart of the great Author of everything, their hearts

---

[2] C. S. Lewis, "The Weight of Glory," in *"The Weight of Glory" and Other Addresses* (New York: HarperCollins, 2001), 1.

never grow weary of it, even if their bodies do. G. K. Chesterton connects the divine dots for us:

> Because children have abounding vitality, because they are in spirit fierce and free, therefore they want things repeated and unchanged. They always say, "Do it again"; and the grown-up person does it again until he is nearly dead. For grown-up people are not strong enough to exult in monotony. But perhaps God is strong enough to exult in monotony. It is possible that God says every morning, "Do it again" to the sun; and every evening, "Do it again" to the moon. It may not be automatic necessity that makes all daisies alike; it may be that God makes every daisy separately, but has never got tired of making them. It may be that He has the eternal appetite of infancy; for we have sinned and grown old, and our Father is younger than we.[3]

So we must rest well by playing hard. We must work hard at resting! The author of Hebrews knows our self-justifying exaltation of works, and he challenges us to channel our efforts into seeing the goodness of pausing:

> So then, there remains a Sabbath rest for the people of God, for whoever has entered God's rest has also rested from his works as God did from his.
> Let us therefore strive to enter that rest . . . (Heb. 4:9–11)

The author of Hebrews knows that getting us to rest can be difficult. He reveals this in his primary focus—getting us to distrust that our work can merit us salvation. And this holds true through the application—trusting that resting well glorifies God and gives witness to the gospel.

We need to remember to play hard. We need to take having fun seriously. This means remembering to do it, for one thing! It means not thinking of rest, play, or fun as beneath us. But it also means being mindful in our rest, play, and fun that these things are gifts

---

[3] Gilbert K. Chesterton, *Orthodoxy* (New York: John Lane, 1908), 108–9.

from God meant to help us celebrate being made in God's image as Creator and project in some way the creative story he is telling with the universe.

This can be difficult to do in the kinds of play that look like battle. It is difficult to do in the kinds of play that involve competition at any level. But this is not because "battle play" and competition are inherently bad. They can actually echo God's story, if we think of them the right way and keep his purposes at the forefront.

Competition in play, for instance, can serve lots of helpful ends. It drives people to work hard to refine the gifts and talents God has given them. It can remind us how fearfully and wonderfully made we are. Reflecting on athletic achievement and competition, Matt Reagan writes:

> God could have created us to be just a pair of eyes, beholding his glory and being perfectly content—but he didn't. He gave us bodies.
>
> The body is a staggering gift, and it enables us to be creators, achievers and accomplishers of remarkable things. In Genesis 1:27–28, God gives humanity the mandate to exercise dominion over the creation, to multiply, and to cultivate the land and its resources. The value of reflecting his beauty through our God-imaging abilities to accomplish is further demonstrated in his call to build the tabernacle with precise and ornate detail, in his later call to build the temple, and in his call to Nehemiah to build the wall, among others. God created us to be creators, and thus reflect him. Building, creating, achieving and accomplishing are good. . . .
>
> Our enjoyment of God in the midst of athletic achievement is a critical component of his glorification.

So if we run fast and enjoy it, which we should, we should enjoy it the way the first frog did. According to Chesterton, the riddle goes like this: "What did the first frog say?" "Lord, how you made me jump!" Jumping and running are enjoyable because they give us the capacity to participate in the beauty and power of God, and they are always gifts from him. As Eric

Liddell memorably said in *Chariots of Fire*, "God made me for a purpose, but he also made me *fast*. And when I run, I feel his pleasure." Perhaps this would be the only legitimate reason for it to be more enjoyable for me to make a jump shot, or run fast, than to watch my friend or teammate do it—just as the Apostle Paul gloried more, it seems, in his experiential participation in the lives of new believers in the early churches than in just hearing about it.[4]

Games of battle play like football and basketball and wrestling, and I would even argue like boxing or mixed martial arts, can glorify God if the hearts of the competitors are in the right place. Battle play, whether it's kids playing war in the neighborhood woods or two pugilists sizing each other up in a title bout, can remind us of lots of noble things: human strength and ability, the war between good and evil, self-discipline and training, and even platform-building for the gospel. (Athletes like A. C. Green, Kurt Warner, and Tim Tebow are good examples of that.)

When used in their proper proportion, sports played hard are a very noble thing. Ray Ortlund writes:

> There is only one way to play football—110% effort every play, all the way to the end of the fourth quarter. You lay it all down on that field. Then you crawl off the field after the final gun with nothing left to give. Football *must* be played with wholehearted abandon. It's the nature of the game. It prepares us for life.
>
> If I could change the Bible, all I would do is add "play high school football" to the qualifications for elders. Men who have experienced such intense effort, hurling themselves into every play, especially as a team sport—such men understand what ministry demands and how *good* it feels to give their all for a cause greater than self.
>
> Of course, there are other ways God provides for men to punch through to the experience of total abandon. Football is

---

[4] Matt Reagan, "March Madness, Athletic Achievement, and Christians in Competitive Sports," *Desiring God* (blog), March 23, 2012, http://www.desiringgod.org/blog/posts/march-madness-athletic-achievement-and-christians-in-competitive-sports/.

not the only way. But every man needs some kind of experience like this, to become the warrior God wants him to be.

There is only one way to serve Christ—all-out passion. Passive men don't understand, men who are afraid they might get knocked down or hurt. Christianity *must* be lived with whole-hearted abandon. It's the nature of the faith. It prepares us for eternity.

Men with a whole heart—joy awaits them![5]

Of course, there are cautions to remember in competitive play, especially in battle play competitions like football or boxing. In relation to the former, Owen Strachan urges sober-mindedness:

Football . . . is physically brutal, and therefore raises concerns for Christians, who of all people have the most stake in human flourishing based on the *imago dei*, the likeness of man to God (Gen. 1:26–27). The game asks a great deal of those who play it, not just in the pros. In terms of concussions alone, taking a shot to the head can leave athletes dazed for days, even weeks. Concussions are the scariest part of the game, and researchers freely confess that they have much to learn about them. It is quite clear that concussions are under-reported and under-diagnosed in youth sports, and despite the millions of small children in football leagues across the country, there are almost no studies of the effects of youth football on the human brain. . . . Football, more than any other mainstream American sport, depends on violence—the cultivation of violent instincts, the use of violence in the moment, and the game yields positive reinforcement after successful acts of violence. Some training in violence is necessary—soldiers defending their country, for example. But the culture of football should concern Christians. The number of football-related arrests, assaults on women and tiny children, murders, drug charges, and more should not glance off the evangelical conscience. The physical brutality of the game likely factors in here. Many of the athletes who have

---

[5] Ray Ortlund, "Men with a Whole Heart," *Christ Is Deeper Still* (blog), July 15, 2010, http://www.thegospelcoalition.org/blogs/rayortlund/2010/07/15/men-with-a-whole-heart/.

gone off the rails and killed themselves and others suffered from CTE. This is not conjecture. It is fact. We kid ourselves if we don't acknowledge the deleterious effect of continuously traumatic contact.[6]

The cautions should be well taken. But should they cause us to reject the thing entirely? Some may argue yes. Some in fact do argue yes as it pertains to competitions like mixed martial arts, and the like. And of course, Christians are free to differ on the moral questions about these certain sports.[7] As Strachan goes on to say, "Football is not impervious to the effects of the curse of Genesis 3. This game is subject to fallenness as all of life is."[8]

So like any good gift God gives, recreation can be misused. Play goes awry when it becomes totally flesh-driven, appetite-driven, and used for our own personal glory and self-satisfaction.

In 2014, after the Seattle Seahawks won the NFC championship game, Seahawk defensive back Richard Sherman, largely considered the best cornerback in the NFL, went on a bit of a rant, saying in part:

> I'm the best corner in the game! When you try me with a sorry receiver like Crabtree, that's the result you're going to get. Don't you ever talk about me. . . . Don't you open your mouth about the best, or I'll shut it for you real quick.[9]

Crabtree was referring to San Francisco 49ers wide receiver Michael Crabtree, whom Sherman guarded most of the game. Later, Sherman called his losing opponent a "mediocre receiver."

When I was a kid, we would call such outbursts "poor sportsmanship." But I was astounded to see many Christians defending Sherman's remarks, referring to the heat of the celebration, the

---

[6] Owen Strachan, "Our Shaken Faith in Football," *Christianity Today* online, September 5, 2013, http://www.christianitytoday.com/ct/2013/september-web-only/our-shaken-faith-in-football.html/.
[7] See, for instance, Matthew Lee Anderson's "The Fatal Tensions of the Fight Churches," *Mere Orthodoxy* (blog), October 8, 2014, http://mereorthodoxy.com/fatal-tensions-fight-churches/.
[8] Strachan, "Our Shaken Faith in Football."
[9] Cindy Boren, "Richard Sherman Goes on Postgame Rant with Erin Andrews," *Early Lead* (blog), *Washington Post*, January 19, 2014, http://www.washingtonpost.com/blogs/early-lead/wp/2014/01/19/richard-sherman-goes-on-postgame-rant-with-erin-andrews-video/.

adrenaline, and so on. Some even argued that the position of cornerback requires such an attitude. But what people interested in the dignity and nobility of sports, what people interested in grace, can easily see is that Sherman, in this instance, was engaging in an honest moment of self-exaltation. His rant was a great example of how not to win.

See, when we use sports poorly, for our own glory and our own sake, we not only lose sorely but win poorly. And athletes, whether they're Christians or not, reflect more the heart of God when they accept responsibility when losing and deflect credit when winning, when they seek the good of their team and the dignity of their opponents, when they do things like give up achievable salaries in order to provide financial advantage for their team in employing more highly skilled players who can benefit the organization. But when an athlete plays only for himself, he loses even if he wins. Many athletes love Philippians 4:13: "I can do all things through him who strengthens me," but would that they'd also take Philippians 2:3 to heart: "Do nothing from selfish ambition or conceit, but in humility count others more significant than yourselves."

Pride affects all of us, and it affects all the ways we play. This is why a lot of us competitive folks need to see the great value in *lightening up*.

When sports go awry, when pride rears its ugly head in our heated moments, as in the stress of competition, the problem is not with the sport. It is with the sportsman.

Paul occasionally used athletic illustrations. A sampling:

An athlete is not crowned unless he competes according to the rules. (2 Tim. 2:5)

Do you not know that in a race all the runners run, but only one receives the prize? So run that you may obtain it. Every athlete exercises self-control in all things. They do it to receive a perishable wreath, but we an imperishable. So I do not run aimlessly; I do not box as one beating the air. But I discipline my body and keep it under control, lest after preaching to others I myself should be disqualified. (1 Cor. 9:24–27)

For while bodily training is of some value, godliness is of value in every way, as it holds promise for the present life and also for the life to come. (1 Tim. 4:8)

Of course, Paul is not directly promoting running and boxing and working out. But by using these things as illustrative examples in promoting spiritual endeavors, he must not find them objectionable in and of themselves. He is drawing out what is good in athletics to point us to the ultimate good of pursuing God's glory. I think most would agree that self-discipline is a good thing and can honor God very much. This is what Paul seems to be aiming at mostly in his references to running, boxing, and training.

Paul probably knows that sports, games, and competition resonate with us because they tap into a profound sense of accomplishment, of reward, and of victory that is found both in God's law and in God's gospel. Just the discipline, the training, and even the pain endured in sports, for instance, can be surprisingly pleasurable. Ray Ortlund writes elsewhere:

It is possible for two psychologies to coexist in our hearts at once—pain and praise. It's like a football player who plays hurt. He feels bad. But he also feels good. Both at the same time. It is so meaningful to be on the team and not in the stands, on the field and not on the bench. A man doesn't mind the two-a-day practices and the wind sprints and the drills and the work and the sweat. He's glad to be playing the game, and not an easy game. That is the very thing that satisfies a man's heart.[10]

Ray is using the pain-enduring football player as an analogy for Christians turning their suffering into praise. But the illustration works for the example of sports and play in general themselves. We were made to work and to rest and to worship, and somehow,

---

[10] Ray Ortlund, "At All Times, Continually," *Christ Is Deeper Still* (blog), January 19, 2011, http://www.thegospelcoalition.org/blogs/rayortlund/2011/01/19/at-all-times-continually/.

in the good gift of however it is you enjoy playing, when thanks is given in it to God, all three of these can exist at once. And the result is deeply satisfying to the God-tuned heart.

Prone to Wonder, Lord I Feel It

Like art, play has no obvious utility. Play is not, as it were, *practical*. And yet, like art, play is somehow necessary. God did not create the world primarily to be practical. He did not create the world solely to be used. He created it to give him glory. And he created us to give him glory. And nothing under heaven is to be considered unnecessary if it can be stewarded to his glory. As Paul says to the young Timothy, "For everything created by God is good, and nothing is to be rejected if it is received with thanksgiving" (1 Tim. 4:4).

One way we receive God's good gifts with thanksgiving is simply by enjoying them, by looking for the joy of God in our use of them. How we rest and play has spiritual substance, because happiness has spiritual purpose. So if Koheleth is right that there is a time for everything under heaven (Eccles. 3:1), then there is definitely a time to laugh, to goof off, to mess around, to be silly. There is a time to nap and to play. There is time for frivolity. It helps us not think so highly of ourselves. Frivolity in the right measure protects us from delusions of sovereignty. If you are never doing nothing, you are wasting your time.

God has made us to wonder.

Do you imagine that heaven will be without play? What if we can play really hard there? We'd be able to do so without fear, without injury. Randy Alcorn ponders:

> We have every reason to believe that the same activities, games, skills, and interests we enjoy here will be available on the New Earth, with many new ones we haven't thought of. (Your favorite sport in Heaven may be one you've never heard of or one that hasn't yet been invented.) . . . What kinds of new sports and activities might we engage in on the New Earth? The possibilities are limitless. Perhaps we'll participate in sports that were

once too risky. And just as we might have stimulating conversations with theologians and writers in Heaven, we might also have the opportunity to play our favorite sports with some of our favorite sports heroes. How would you like to, in your resurrection body, play golf with Payne Stewart or play basketball with David Robinson? How would you like to play catch with Andy Pettitte or go for a run with Jesse Owens or Eric Liddell?[11]

Because the gifts of rest and play were given that we might reflect on and revel in the creative artistry of God, it makes sense that this reflection and reveling will continue into the age to come. But we will rest without the sin of laziness and we will play without the sins of pride, malice, greed, or any other corrupting thing. We will rest and play and feel God's pleasure. Anticipating that ought to affect our rest and play on *this* side of heaven.

Recently I saw a sports documentary segment on a six-year-old Australian girl named Quincy Symonds. Quincy is a surfing prodigy. When she was four, her father took her out surfing for the first time. She got up on just her second wave. Since then, she has only increased in her abilities, and everyone who knows anything about surfing will tell you that what Quincy can do at her age in the ocean is very special. She doesn't just have a good sense of balance and athletic ability. She has a gift. One of the narrators of the film describes her sense of awareness in the ocean and her easy way with the surf as a sixth sense. She has something that most people do not, that even most surfers do not.

But Quincy also has a rare condition called congenital adrenal hyperplasia. When she gets hurt, even in a minor way, her body does not produce the cortisol that most human bodies produce to help them compensate and recover from injury. So even a minor injury or illness can endanger her life. A few times after becoming hurt, Quincy's parents got her to the hospital with minutes to spare. Her mother often keeps watch while Quincy is surfing, an emer-

---

[11] Randy Alcorn, *Heaven* (Wheaton, IL: Tyndale, 2004), 410–11.

gency kit in hand. If not treated immediately, Quincy could literally die from falling down too hard.

The documentary covers some of the criticism Quincy's parents and coaches have heard. They are taking a great risk. (And when Quincy isn't surfing, she's skateboarding!) But you watch this little girl surf—and I know nothing about surfing—and her look of sheer joy is so evident. She seems both extraordinary in skill and overwhelmed with satisfaction. Her coach, professional surfer Anthony Hope, has said:

> There were a lot of surfers looking at me like, "You shouldn't be out here with that tiny kid." . . . However, after pushing her into a perfect 3-foot wave, she took off down the line, tearing the wave up. I was shocked, speechless and super excited. I knew immediately she was something very special.[12]

God has gifted Quincy with a very rare talent. I don't know if the Symonds family are believers in Christ or not, but it seems likely that when Quincy surfs, she feels God's pleasure. As the father of two little girls, I understand the fear that might outweigh the desire to let her feel God's pleasure in using that gift.

And yet, she seems made for it. And there is a time for everything.

---

[12] Jeffrey Donovan, "6-Year-Old Surfer Girl Won't Let Disease Wipe Out Her Serious Skills," *Today Health* online, August 22, 2014, http://www.today.com/health/6-year-old-surfer-girl-quincy-symonds -nicknamed-flying-squirrel-1D80101122/.

9

Love Story

God's Plan for Romance, Marriage, and Sex

It's not often that Hollywood gets anything about relationships, men, women, dating, sex, or marriage right, but occasionally a filmmaker will give us a rare, honest peek behind the curtain. One of the most iconic examples is at the end of Mike Nichols's 1967 film *The Graduate*. I'm not necessarily recommending the movie to you, and most of you who've at least heard of it likely know it is mainly about a recent college grad (played by Dustin Hoffman) who carries on an affair with an older married woman. But by the end of the movie, Dustin realizes he's actually "in love" with the woman's daughter.

The only problem is that the daughter is supposed to marry another guy. So you have this big dramatic scene at the end of the movie where the wedding is about to take place and Dustin Hoffman is racing to the church in his little convertible and Simon and Garfunkel's "Mrs. Robinson" is playing on the soundtrack, but then he runs out of gas and he has to run the rest of the way to the church and he finally gets there and the lady and her groom-to-be are at the altar celebrating their first wedded kiss and the priest is about to pronounce them man and wife and there's suddenly Dustin Hoffman banging on the glass windows overlooking the sanctuary, crying out her name, "Elaine! Elaine! Elaine!" And the girl turns and sees him and realizes she's in love with him too and she leaves her groom at the altar and runs away in her wedding dress to be with Dustin Hoffman and they get on a bus and ride away into the sunset.

Countless romantic movies have copied this scene, where the wedding gets interrupted by "true love" or the gal breaks up with her boring boyfriend to get with the charming romantic lead of the movie (usually Tom Hanks, right?). But in *The Graduate*, we see something different. Dustin Hoffman and his runaway bride get on that bus all smiles and happiness and exuberant rebellion, and they sit in the back, and the camera just sits there on them and holds. And it holds and it holds. And gradually their faces turn from nervous smiles to blank expressions. And there's no emotion there at all. It's almost as if the reality of what they've done has just hit them, and the reality of an uncertain future is just now settling in, and the camera just sits there watching them stare off into the distance with coldness on their faces. And that's how the movie ends.

Not very romantic. But a lot more realistic, especially in the world where romance has gone awry. But God is not finished with it yet.

Love's Beginning

The story God is telling about romance begins with the first song in the Bible, which happens to be a love song. Adam takes a look at the newly formed Eve and busts out the poetry:

> This at last is bone of my bones
>   and flesh of my flesh;
> she shall be called Woman,
>   because she was taken out of Man. (Gen. 2:23)

Adam's pure, uninhibited smittenness with Eve gives way to their pure, uninhibited union with each other. Man and woman, "therefore" (Gen. 2:24), leave their single life, surrender their dependence on family, and join together in marriage. They are "naked and unashamed" (2:25).

It begins with a kind of marveling. Adam and Eve are basking in God's creative artistry and his creative purposes. The story he's telling seems extraordinarily pleasing to them. But they want to tell their own story soon enough.

When God comes to pronounce the curse for their disobedience in Genesis 3, he doesn't just announce the disconnect between mankind and God, he announces the disconnect within mankind. The woman will tend to "desire" her husband in idolatrous ways and the man will tend to "rule" over his wife in prideful ways (Gen. 3:16).

When we try to write our own stories with our lives, including our romances and marriages, we not only quench our sensitivity to God's sovereign story, but we actually crowd out the people we mean to include in our storylines. Jesus says to love our neighbor as ourselves. This is what happens when he's in the center of our lives. But when we make ourselves the hero, our neighbors always play supporting parts to our own self-exaltation projects. And we end up not loving them. The bitter truth is that sometimes these neighbors are our spouses, our children, those closest to us. The self-centered spouse is the marriage-stifling spouse.

Genesis 2 explains why romance is so awesome, and Genesis 3 explains why romance is so complicated. It explains why, when the heat of attraction cools, we are left sitting in the back of the bus like Dustin Hoffman and his bride, feeling the weight of reality sinking in.

Matt Chandler writes:

> When the beauty fades, what integrity will remain?
>
> We can always adjust our outer appearance. Our culture has advanced in the ways of makeup and hairstyles and beauty products, but we've also added cosmetic surgery, health-food culture, and fitness programs bordering on cults. We don't all

look great, but we can all look a little "better" with a little work. But the inner us? That will come out. We can't hide it forever. In times of intimacy, in times of stress, in times of struggle, there's no putting makeup on a terrible personality. There's no cosmetic surgery for poverty of character.

You can't hide that inner you. It's the real you.[1]

When we first meet someone we're attracted to, even as we get to know them better and even if they become the person we date, get engaged to, and marry, the initial days of romance are spent so much on image management and projection. The longer a courtship endures, the more reality we see, of course. But it's usually not until a bit into marriage that we begin to realize what love actually costs. Which is why so many marriages don't make it past the seven-year mark.

When God calls Adam and Eve on the carpet over their disobedience, the first thing Adam does is blame Eve, and the first thing Eve does is blame the Serpent. Neither will own up to the fact that they are not the hero of the story. They play the victim; they cannot fathom their own villainy. And this same game plays out daily in households around the world.

We keep looking for connection and significance, and we sense (rightly) that there is something in the realities of romance and love that satisfies these needs. But we tend not to hear what romance and love are actually saying about connection and significance because we are too busy loudly broadcasting what we *want* them to say. But for those with sensitive ears, the love song of grace helps. God is telling a story with us and for us in our romantic relationships, but it is not ultimately about us. It is about himself.

Love's Covenant

I think one of the reasons so many marriages fail is that we forget just what marriage *is*. We recite vows at our weddings, we have

---

[1] Matt Chandler with Jared C. Wilson, *The Mingling of Souls: God's Design for Love, Marriage, Sex, and Redemption* (Colorado Springs: David C. Cook, 2015), 34–35.

1 Corinthians 13 read aloud, we even have our ceremonies in a church, but we haven't adequately prepared ourselves for what being married is *for*.

We are thinking happiness and romance, and those are great things that every marriage should have in them, but when we set our sights solely on happiness and romance, we actually weaken our marriage, not strengthen it. Because happiness and romance are fluid things. They are contingent on our feelings. What happens if your marriage is built on feelings?

The story that God is telling with the world calls us back to a radical reshaping of what we think marriage is for. Personal happiness and romantic fulfillment can be the by-products of a healthy marriage, but the husband's and wife's primary purpose in marriage is not happiness and romance. The primary purpose of marriage is giving God glory by bearing witness to the gospel. The primary purpose of marriage is to make Jesus look big.

This is why the apostle Paul says things like:

> Wives, submit to your own husbands, *as to the Lord*. (Eph. 5:22)

> Husbands, love your wives, *as Christ loved the church*. (5:25)

> For no one ever hated his own flesh, but nourishes and cherishes it, *just as Christ does the church*. (5:29)

Paul keeps bringing what the husband and wife are doing back to Christ. When God gave us marriage, he gave it not just for our happiness, but for a living example of worship of him. Gary Thomas, the author of *Sacred Marriage*, says:

> Most people today think that their greatest need is to be loved, that is why they get married. They want to find someone that will love them, they want to be noticed, they feel lonely, they want to be appreciated. The biblical view is that God has met that need. He proved His love for us through Christ, He will love us, He will accept us. So your greatest need has already been met. The greatest need now then is to learn how to love.

I look at marriage as a teacher of how to love. If you are married to a person with a temper, how do you learn to love a person with a temper? If you are married to a person who is overly sensitive or selfish, how do you learn to love a sensitive or selfish person?

Well, it is really through humility, realizing that I am not like Christ. We compare ourselves to Charlie Sheen and Mike Tyson and say, "Well I am not Mike Tyson, I am not Charlie Sheen but I am not Jesus either." So even though a person might be more spiritual than their spouse they still realize the need to grow in how they love their spouse. So then the things I used to resent about my marriage—now I see it as a purpose of my marriage, as I now see that God designed it to pinch my feet, to show me that I am selfish and that I don't know how to love, to show me that I am not like Christ so I can become better at how I love.[2]

This is an important refocus for us, because what Thomas is getting at is very much what happens when we read important Bible passages like Ephesians 5:22–33 through the lens of the gospel. When we read the biblical texts on marriage through the narrative lens of self-centeredness, we tend to read them like this: "Hmm, it says here, 'Husbands, love your wives as Christ loved the church.' Yep, yep, sounds good; all set there. 'Wives, submit to your husbands.' Oh, well, now! Have you seen this, honey?"

Reading the Bible as a story primarily about us is to generally see in it what applies *to everybody else.* We need the deep humility of that secret of the universe—the gospel of grace.

I think the heaviness of Ephesians 5's words on marriage speaks to the primary ways marriage works to help us glorify Christ in the gospel, and part of that work is the deep scouring it does of our souls. If we have the eyes to see, marriage does a great job of revealing our idols.

Let's just take the common scenario of the messy kitchen. Some

---

[2] Edward Lee, "Conversation with Best Selling Christian Author, Gary Thomas—Part 1," *Intersections* online (January 22, 2012), https://crossingintersections.wordpress.com/2012/01/22/conversation-with-gary-thomas/.

of this may have to do with the stereotypical ideas of women liking things tidy and men not caring about messes, but a lot of it has to do with how you were raised, how your own mom and dad acted in the home, etc. So a couple gets married and the wife comes from a home that was very tidy and Mom cleaned a lot but everybody else tidied up too and picked up after themselves. The husband came from a home where Mom did all the tidying up, and everybody else's job was to make messes for Mom to tidy up. Now you see, neither husband nor wife got married expecting to ruin each other's lives over the cleanliness of the kitchen. They just brought their own values and upbringing into the home. They had different expectations. So husband is making messes, assuming wife will clean them up. And wife is wondering how husband can be so callous as to not pick up after himself.

Now we're at a fault line. And it happens in a million different scenarios in all of our marriages. We bring the weight of expectations, of personal preferences, of different values and interests and personalities, and we expect the other to give more. The kitchen is messy now. Wife is angry. She starts nagging, complaining, withholding affection, and giving guilt trips. Husband is stubborn, aloof, lazy, and not going to respond to nagging.

Idols have been revealed. Our individual storylines are on vivid display. The wife's expectation that her husband will pick up after himself is not unreasonable or wrong, but her reactions are becoming more and more graceless. Why? Because she loves a clean kitchen more than she loves her husband. The husband's original expectation that his wife act just like his mom is somewhat natural, but now he knows differently and so to dig in his heels and fail to honor his wife's preferences is selfish. He loves his own comfort and pride more than he loves his wife.

But being honest about these inner bents and this outer bitterness is how marriage can become hugely sanctifying if we'll open our hearts to the reality of what conflicts and stresses reveal about ourselves. So, husbands, are you reading Ephesians 5 and thinking, "I hope she takes this to heart"? Wives, are you reading Ephesians 5 and thinking, "Why doesn't my husband do this?" Right now, are you thinking, "Boy, I hope my spouse is really paying attention to this paragraph"?

Pride is being revealed.

Or when you come up against the call to give of yourself, to submit, to sacrifice, to love selflessly, are you thinking of all the reasons why this doesn't mean what it says? That it doesn't exactly apply to you? That if Paul only knew about *your* marriage, he wouldn't have written the things he did? That God surely meant to exempt you from this design?

Idols are being revealed.

What do we do with this mess? It's a recipe for disaster. I have long said that I think every day of marriage is like a repeat of those moments right after the fall. Adam and Eve are standing there vulnerable and broken, each wanting to pin the blame on the other.

When the gospel is applied to romantic love, it results for most in what we call the covenant of marriage. And it is important to think of marriage as a covenant. It helps us guard against self-centeredness. Chandler again:

> Since we are sinners, our natural responses in relationships usually hinge on what might be gained. We tend to turn all our relationships into contractual arrangements of some kind. We'll sacrifice for our spouse if she deserves it. We'll submit to our spouse if he agrees with us. We'll serve our spouse if she'll serve us in return. But these kinds of thoughts bear no resemblance to the gracious covenant God makes with us. . . .
>
> In the covenant of marriage, husband and wife give themselves to each other. It's not fifty-fifty; it's one hundred–one hundred. At any given time either spouse won't have 100 percent to give, but this does not diminish the other's commitment because they are not in a contract but a covenant. As in the covenant of grace initiated by God to save sinners, one party can give 100 percent even if the other gives nothing.[3]

---

[3] Chandler with Wilson, *The Mingling of Souls*, 103–4.

And what are we giving? What are the "plot points" in God's covenantal story about marriage? Here's the role of the wife in the narrative:

> Wives, submit to your own husbands, as to the Lord. For the husband is the head of the wife even as Christ is the head of the church, his body, and is himself its Savior. Now as the church submits to Christ, so also wives should submit in everything to their husbands. (Eph. 5:22–24)

Now, "as to the Lord" implies a few things, and we should note this means no wife ought to submit to sin or abuse (which is sin). The Lord doesn't abuse or otherwise sin.

But it also implies something we often would rather get around. See, when we submit to the Lord, we often do so without knowing what the outcome will be. Sometimes we do it without agreeing that his way is best. The word *submit*, in fact, kind of entails that we might do things differently if he weren't in charge.

Of course, no husband is close to the perfect decision-maker that Jesus is. (Can I get an Amen?)

But God has designed marriage to work with husbands at the head (as in 5:23). And he knows full well that wives won't always agree with their husbands or trust their husbands or even *like* their husbands. And this is why he doesn't say, "Submit to your own husbands, because they are so awesome and always make good choices."

No, he brings in the perspective of Christ so that a wife will know that submitting to her husband shows faith in God's design. It may all pan out very terribly, as many husbands' plans often do. But again, terrible outcomes can be God's plan for sanctifying us, helping us become more like Jesus.

Now, as heavy a burden as it may seem for wives to submit to their husbands, the plot point for the husband even more explicitly highlights the cross:

> Husbands, love your wives, as Christ loved the church and gave himself up for her that he might sanctify her, having cleansed her

by the washing of water with the word, so that he might present the church to himself in splendor, without spot or wrinkle or any such thing, that she might be holy and without blemish. (5:25–27)

How did Christ love the church? He "gave himself up for her." He was self-emptying. Tender. Loving. Patient. Relentlessly gracious. He was a servant!

Now, it's the Holy Spirit's work to spiritually sanctify a wife, but he works through a Christlike husband. The aim is the sanctification of the wife, not the exploitation of her. A husband's treatment of his wife should make her clean, not dirty! Introducing her to porn is out. Cheating on her is out. Demeaning her is out. Picking on her is out. Dishonoring her is out.

Now who's doing what starts getting mixed up here. (We are heading to that mystery pronouncement in Eph. 5:32.) Who is washing whom with the water of the word? Is Christ washing the church or the husband washing his wife? Both. The picture given is that just as Jesus loves the church and "gospels" her, husbands are to love their wives and "gospel" them. And if you're unclear on what this means, I will break it down more specifically:

Most women—I hesitate to say all women, but nearly all women—are starving for approval, for a feeling of acceptance and desirability, for security, for being totally known and at the same time totally loved. This is their hunger for connection and significance. And this is what the gospel provides in the declaration of justification.

In a similar way, then, it is a husband's Christian duty not to weigh his wife down with law—with expectations, with disapprovals, with duties, with disappointment, with rejection. It is a husband's Christian duty to liberate his wife with gospel—with approval, with acceptance, with freedom, with delight. It is a husband's job to rehearse his wife's justification.

So the marriage union is unlike any other, and Paul roots his teaching right back in the original love story when he quotes

Genesis 2:24 in Ephesians 5:31: "Therefore a man shall leave his father and mother and hold fast to his wife, and the two shall become one flesh."

The gospeled marriage is built on this "one-flesh" relationship that God established before the fall. It's a covenantal union where two become one. This is why God says don't separate it. This is why God hates divorce. It's like ripping something. It's tearing apart. And because the fall came *after* the covenant, when the effects of the fall make themselves apparent in our marriages, we have to go back before the fall to God's gracious covenant. What was the foundation of our marriage? Not that we'd always be happy, not that we'd always have things easy, not that it'd be lollipops and rainbows all the livelong day, but that God put us together to glorify him. And for some reason he determined that loving sinners most glorifies him.

If we want our marriages to follow God's storyline, we will take to heart what God is saying here about husbands and wives and one-fleshedness and sacrifice and submission and respect and cherishing. Because God knows what he's talking about. He designed the thing. And it's not like he didn't anticipate all the reasons we'd come up with to explain why these admonitions don't exactly apply to our situations. Like, we all know we're married to sinners, but couldn't have God given us a, you know, *less sinny* sinner to be married to?

But this is exactly what marriage is for. This is what the marriage vows are for. You don't really even need that "for better" stuff in there, that "in richness" and "in health" stuff. Nobody in their right mind is bailing during the good times. No, the vows are for the other stuff. "For worse." "In poverty." "In sickness." The vows exist because sin is real. Sure, we may not know *what sins* will become real in our relationships, putting stress on the covenant, but the vows exist because sin does.

The vow of the gospel exists because sin does.

See, the story of Christ and his bride is very messy. Very difficult.

It is a sordid history, to be sure. One of the most vivid illustrations we get is that of the prophet Hosea, who was commanded by God to take a prostitute for a wife. As she keeps cheating on him and prostituting herself, Hosea stays faithful through all the pain, the heartache, the dishonor, the confusion. He stays faithful. Why? Because God had joined them together. And because God in his astounding wisdom and artistry was showing Hosea—and us—what it is like for Christ to love his church.

When we stand at the altar making our vows, we really don't think the bad will be that bad. We expect sin but not *that kind*. But our holy bridegroom Jesus Christ makes his vow knowing full well what he's forgiving. He knows us inside and out. He knows what we're guilty of and what we *will be* guilty of. He knows just how awful it's going to get.

Every day, you and I reject the holiness of Jesus in a million different ways, only a fraction of which are we conscious of. If Jesus were keeping a list of our wrongs, none of us would stand a chance. At any second of any day, even on our best days, Jesus could have the legal grounds to say, "Enough of this. I can't do it anymore. You've violated my love for the last time."

The truth is, you've never met a wronged spouse like Jesus. You've never met a disrespected spouse like Jesus. You've never met a spouse who more than carried their weight like Jesus. He's carrying the entire relationship on his back. This thing is totally one-sided.

And yet: He loves. And he gives. And he serves. And he approves. And he washes. And he delights. And he romances. And he doesn't just tolerate us; he lavishes his affection on us. He justifies and sanctifies and glorifies.

I don't know what you come away from Ephesians 5:22–33 thinking. Maybe you read it and think, "Sacrifice? Submit? No way. I can't do this."

Husbands are thinking, "I cannot sacrifice for her."

Wives are thinking, "I cannot submit to him."

And we can't—at least, not the way God wants us to.

But God knows this. He knows we are terrible obeyers. He knows we are self-interested sacrificers and stubborn submitters. And he gave up his life for us anyway. He died to forgive all our sins and rose again that we might never have them held against us.

Be still, our beating hearts. Here's a groom worth swooning over.

> I will establish my covenant with you, and you shall know that I am the LORD, that you may remember and be confounded, and never open your mouth again because of your shame, when I atone for you for all that you have done, declares the Lord GOD. (Ezek. 16:62–63)

What kind of story is this, anyway?

Koheleth's secret identity tells us:

> Three things are too wonderful for me;
>   four I do not understand:
> the way of an eagle in the sky,
>   the way of a serpent on a rock,
> the way of a ship on the high seas,
>   and the way of a man with a virgin. (Prov. 30:18–19)

He's so "twitterpated," he can't even get his math straight!

Paul tells us. Marriage is a "profound mystery" (Eph. 5:32), but it's about Jesus and his bride, the church.

This is why when Christ finally returns to consummate his kingdom and redeem his bride into glory, we won't need marriage anymore. All our messy marriages will be fulfilled in him.

But there are mysteries within the mystery. We should expect a brilliant story like the gospel to work like that. Sex is one of those inner mysteries. God's story does, after all, account for everything.

Love's Consummation

Belgian Catholic Archbishop André-Joseph Léonard was once speaking to a university group in Brussels on the topic of freedom of expression and blasphemy, when a group of topless feminist protestors with slogans scrawled across their torsos invaded the space and began taunting the man and dousing him with water. They had the water in little bottles shaped like the Virgin Mary. They meant ostensibly to protest the Catholic Church's stances on homosexuality, and they targeted Archbishop Léonard in particular because he has been fairly outspoken about the issue, most recently confirming for a Belgian newspaper that a Christian praxis for homosexuals should involve celibacy.

The scene was a very stark and disturbing one, and very powerful. Several newspapers ran photos, obscuring the protestors' breasts of course. But what you see are four angry women in various states of rancor dousing this man, who is seated, with water, while the man himself sits quietly, hands folded, eyes closed, praying. I don't know anything else beyond this incident about Archbishop Léonard, but the image reminded me of the mental image of our Lord enduring, absorbing the taunts of his tormentors without saying a word.

Now, what were these nice ladies protesting? The Catholic Church's position on homosexuality, yes, but something else more fundamental. I think we see in this scene a growing everyday occurrence for most of the post-Christendom West, but in the spiritual sense, a battle you and I wage every day of our lives. We see the fundamental protest in slogans like "Get the Government Out of the Bedroom" and "My Body; My Choice" and—as I see from many on Twitter and Facebook on an almost daily basis now—"Don't Judge Me."

What people protest, I believe, is authority. We all want, in our flesh, life without restraint. "You're not the boss of me," we say. And is there anything moderns try to write our own stories with these days more than sexuality?

We can't help but see external authority as stifling, discouraging, and disempowering. I think largely, even in church cultures, we have trouble with authority not simply because often people in authority are authoritarian or simply poor leaders but because we have no vision of the gospel that helps us see authority as a blessing. And in the areas of gender roles and sex, one glaring weakness in many egalitarian arguments is the failure to grapple with biblical authority. This is why you see so much egalitarianism in the progressive Christian world coming alongside affirmation of gay marriage, the rejection of the inerrancy of Scripture, the muddling of male and female roles in home and church leadership, and the like. At its root, it is a resentment of authority that might keep us from doing what we want.

But seeing authority through the eyes of the gospel? Now that would be wisdom.

"Where there is no prophetic vision the people cast off restraint, but blessed is he who keeps the law" (Prov. 29:18). This verse is much misused. Some pastors use it to cudgel others into their big ideas for ministry strategy. But the reality is not so flexible: without a word from God, people will do what is right in their own eyes. But it is a blessing—a balm to life—to live God's way, to subject everything under heaven to the command of the Author.

In 1 Corinthians 7:1–5 Paul applies the secret of the universe to one of life's great mysteries—sex. He begins by addressing the Corinthian church's original question sent to him: "Now concerning the matters about which you wrote: 'It is good for a man not to have sexual relations with a woman'" (v. 1). He is likely citing their dangerously Gnostic overreaction to the avoidance of fornication and sexual defilement.

The question Paul appears to be addressing demonstrates the church's imbalanced approach to authority that stifles the spirit of the laws against sex outside of the marriage covenant. They are in danger of "falling off the horse on the other side." We see this overreach of authority—authority that stifles—throughout church history's treatment of even sex *within* marriage. For instance, it is said that Clement of Alexandria taught that you can have sex only at night, and you shouldn't enjoy it. Origen considered sex so sinful, he castrated himself. In the Middle Ages, the church forbade sex between married couples up to 252 days of the year, leaving just 83 when it was permitted, assuming the woman was not menstruating, pregnant, or had just given birth. But you could still couldn't enjoy it. Today, we suggest to our young people that sex is dirty, gross, and dangerous, and then we tell them to have fun with it in marriage. It's no wonder we find ourselves more than a little confused.

Is that God's design? Is that the design behind Genesis 2:25? "The man and his wife were both naked and were not ashamed."

That's not where Paul goes at all. The Corinthians were essentially asking, "Paul, we've heard that because of immorality it's good just to not have sex at all. Help us out. What do you say?" Paul says, "But because of the temptation to sexual immorality, each man should have his own wife and each woman her own husband" (7:2).

He's giving us the framework for sexual intimacy, the boundaries, the outline for the story. He wants us to know that God has designated marriage as the context for sinless sex.

Marriage is the context for sinless sex. The laws then give us parameters. There are laws against adultery but also divorce; there are instructions about sexual behavior but also lustful thoughts.

Why did God give us these laws? Is he just a cosmic killjoy?

No. Because marriage is meant to be a picture of the gospel, and because the gospel is glorious and eternal, marriage is meant to be weighty and permanent. We make marriage—and thus, sex—about us, but God says they're primarily about Christ.

We see this in the way we've turned marriage into a sentimental, romantic relationship rather than a covenantal union, just as we see it in the way we've turned sex into a tool for self-gratification rather than as a way of serving our spouses by nourishing and cherishing them. We see it in how we distinguish family from marriage, as when same-sex marriage advocates argue that "anybody makes a family."

And while I know it's a touchy subject, can there be much doubt that when we divorced sex even philosophically from the prospect of procreation—and more generally, the flourishing of a family—we implicitly acknowledged that our sex is self-worship?

I'm not a so-called "quiverfull" proponent—my wife and I have two children, not ten—and I am not against the use of all methods of family planning (and you'll notice that Paul, like the Song of Solomon, says nothing here about procreation, which he well likely should have if sex is primarily for having children), but marital sex is inextricably tied to the flourishing of whole families, which of course includes the creation mandate of being fruitful and multiplying.

The marriage institution and its covenant and the family unit and its flourishing are good, helpful guides for marital sexuality. When married couples have a sex life *with each other*—certainly not with another person, but also not with their own minds, such as with a computer in the darkness of the study, and not with romance novels or soap operas or tabloid magazines—they are honoring their one-fleshedness and investing in the radiant joy of their families.

Ever seen married couples who have lived like platonic roommates over a length of time? Look at their kids. Do they often look happy? They may not *know* their parents aren't enjoying romance, of course, but they kinda do. There is something about moms and dads being in love with each other that makes kids feel safe, secure, happy, and loved themselves.

Paul then applies the gracious covenant of marriage to sexuality when he writes:

> The husband should give to his wife her conjugal rights, and likewise the wife to her husband. For the wife does not have authority over her own body, but the husband does. Likewise the husband does not have authority over his own body, but the wife does. (1 Cor. 7:3–4)

Here is explicit authority talk. As it pertains to our bodies, mutual submission means our spouse has authority over us. But notice that the burden of responsibility is on the giver of rights, not the assumer of them. In other words, Paul is telling married persons to make it their responsibility to give to their spouses their conjugal rights, not make sure their spouses are giving them theirs.

It's a subtle point but an important one. What happens in a marriage when two people are always concerned about what they each "deserve"?

Paul says, "You each serve the other," as if each has authority over the other. What a beautiful romantic picture of Romans 12:10: "Outdo one another in showing honor." And if joy comes through Christlikeness, as the Scriptures promise, there can be nothing more joyful than giving my wife authority over my body as an act of sacrifice and service to her.

The key here, of course, is mutuality. If I have authority over her body but she does not have authority over mine, we don't have the beautiful stalemate of covenantal grace and a picture of the complementary truths in the multifaceted person of the glorious Christ, but instead a legalistic relationship, a harmful one—for her and eventually even for me.

We also notice that Paul uses the word "rights" in this passage. The husband should give to his wife her conjugal rights, and likewise the wife to her husband. "Rights" implies a variety of desires *and nondesires*. This means I am giving my wife the right to have sex with me. But I also give her the right to say, "Not tonight, honey. It's been a long day and I'm really tired. I want to love you that way, but let's try for tomorrow night." It means I am giving my wife the right to be sick or otherwise distressed or just flat-out disinterested without pressure from me to "give me *my* rights."

This view of authority and conjugal rights is vitally important for a Christlike marriage, especially in marriages when a spouse may be dealing with trauma from abuse, recovery from illnesses, or just completely unable to enjoy intercourse (perhaps even ever) due to a disability or other preventative condition. We all know that sex is not marriage; so let's all remember that marriage isn't sex.

Giving our spouse the conjugal right to not have sex with us is a picture of authority that embodies the wisdom of the gospel because it seeks the good of the other, not chiefly the pleasure of itself. Because that's not love, is it?

So the grace-driven way to look at this passage, the way that computes with God's overarching narrative about everything, is not that we have authority over our spouse's body but that they have authority over ours. Without the grace of God motivating us and empowering us, in fact, this sort of stalemate of rights and desires becomes the recipe for disaster.

Only freedom in Christ creates the freedom to give up seeking my rights and set about seeking justice for yours. If I am hidden with Christ in God, I have nothing left to hide, and if I'm secured in Christ, I have nothing left to protect. I consider myself dead, in fact, and live only in Christ, so I can pursue my wife's good and her pleasure and her flourishing—and she mine—only because God has set us free in Christ from sin and shame.

And this of course is true for a holistic view of marital sexuality, not just what's going on between the sheets. (This is the story of *everything*, after all!) For instance, why do I work out? Or to be more accurate: *when* I work out, why do I work out? Not because I want to look great. I gave up on that a long time ago! When I exercise, I do it because I know it honors my wife's desire that I steward my body and be around a while for her and our children. She has authority over my body and so I go to the gym because my body is not mine to waste. It belongs to her. And I want her to see I'm honoring her with it.

But before my body is hers—and before hers is mine—before mine is mine and hers is hers, I am, in the words of the Heidelberg Catechism, "not my own, but belong—body and soul, in life and in death—to my faithful Savior Jesus Christ." And, "Because I belong to him, Christ, by his Holy Spirit, assures me of eternal life and makes me wholeheartedly willing and ready from now on to live for him."[4]

---

[4] Heidelberg Catechism, q. 1.

This is how Paul reflects the authorship of God in marital sexuality:

Do not deprive one another, except perhaps by agreement for a limited time, that you may devote yourselves to prayer; but then come together again, so that Satan may not tempt you because of your lack of self-control. (1 Cor. 7:5)

Paul puts marital sex right on the spiritual plane. He gives it a spiritual import. This is weighty business. This is spiritual warfare! (I don't remember reading this in the Frank Peretti novels that shaped so much of my generation's thinking on spiritual warfare.)

This is of paramount importance to the complementarian view that God has placed sex within the sphere of spiritual defense—filled in its abstinence by prayer (not by taking up kickboxing or pottery) and used in its presence as an escape from temptation, as a way of placing himself right there in the bedroom with us. Sex was God's idea. The multifunctional body parts were God's idea. The nerve endings were God's idea. The reason this is important for the complementarian viewpoint is because it reminds us that there is authority and submission in the bedroom as a reflection of our submission together to the authority of God.

Complementarians screw this up when they assume that marital sex ought to be tuned to the sexual appetites of the husband because he is the leader of the home and his wife is supposed to submit to him. But that's telling the husband's story with sex. And egalitarians screw this up when they assume that if both parties consent to something, that is the end of the matter. That's telling the world's story with sex.

It is possible to have consensual sex in marriage that dishonors God and each other. Even married couples can have sex in an ungodly manner. The marriage covenant does not sanctify every appetite. And not even consent baptizes every sexual act.

Mutual consent is a minimum, of course. But there is a God, and neither husband nor wife is he.

Just because a husband and wife may agree to use pornography

in their sexual foreplay or agree to add bondage to their sexual rep-
ertoire or assume that any orifice constitutes a sexual opportunity
does not mean these acts are consistent with sex that honors God,
let alone that honors each other.

It would be just like Satan to tarnish even the great freedom
of expression we have in the marital bedroom. Think of the ways
many read Song of Solomon, for instance, as if it were a sex manual.
As if sex were just about body parts. Like it's supposed to be read
like IKEA furniture instructions.

No, it's *poetry*. Romantic, sexually sensual poetry, yes, but poetry. When Adam first saw Eve, he did not blurt out some blunt
sexual blather; he sang a song. That's an instinct, really, not an
"obedience." It was a praise response to the beheld beauty. In Proverbs 5:19, the young man is told to always rejoice in the wife of his
youth, to let her breasts fill him with delight at all times. This means
that the "easy" joy of the newlywed disposition is to be pursued,
cultivated, and felt throughout married life. But delight gets harder
to come by through years of familiarity and conflict. As delight gets
scarcer, the wisdom of the gospel must fill the space.

How does the gospel give us this wisdom? How does the gospel
help me to delight in my wife twenty years into our marriage in the
way I delighted in her twenty minutes into it? How does the gospel
help me to cultivate the instinctual response of enjoying her breasts
now (and into the future) as I did then? It happens by remembering the secret of the universe, remembering God's modus operandi
in the world.

When I see myself in the light of God's holiness, I see how unworthy and unattractive I really am. And then I see that God, despite his perfect perfection and my rebellious imperfection, loves
me totally and eternally, to the point of giving himself up for me
in the sending of his Son to die for me. That now, though I am an
undeserving sinner, I am an eternally justified saint. That in fact,
God rejoices over me. That I, who deserve the condemnation of
death and hell, am the apple of his eye.

Knowing all of that and more, then, with what right do I have to look at my wife with anything but approval and delight? It would be an affront to the gospel, a fist shaken at God to not delight in my wife at all times. And the beauty is that this instinct becomes more natural because it is supernatural, something that the Spirit develops in us the more we pursue marveling at the gospel of Jesus Christ. The more we stare with care at the glory of Christ, the more like him we will become.

And so in all the fun that sex is—or rather, can be—let us remember that it is making love, not simply making orgasms. Marital sex is expression of love for and service to each other in a reflection of the care and forethought and patience and joy Christ has given his bride.

We see the rotten fruit of casting off authority in our culture. We are seeing more and more a reflection of the ruthless degradation rampant in the book of Judges, where we are told more than once that this is the result of every man doing what is right in his own eyes. That sort of living is foolishness. The declaration that "only God can judge me" is foolishness, especially since so many who say that go on living as if God *won't*.

But wisdom about sex means embracing the authority of God, and all that that authority means.

Our sex is so awkward, really. It is a great grace that God has given it to us but a great grace that we can be so bad at something that is still so helpful for the building up of our marriages, the health of our families, the endurance and stability of the marital institution in society, the joy even of our churches, and the glory of Christ Jesus. *If* we will put a stake in the heart of our self-sovereignty and embrace the gracious yoke of God's sovereign story.

Love's Legacy

With our marriages and with our sex, we are hopefully making families. Ideally, our romances are cultivating legacies of love and joy long after death has done us part.

Soon after Adam and Eve's marriage gets poisoned by sin, their family bears rotten fruit. In Genesis 4, their son Cain murders his brother Abel. It's the first example of the sins of the father being visited upon his children.

And we see early on how Cain's anger and self-interest set his own descendants on a course of destruction and faithlessness. Lamech is just the highlight of the lowlights resulting. He starts singing his own prideful song. Cain's descendants showed great promise— they weren't poor, they weren't stupid, they weren't untalented. They just made self-centered decisions and positioned themselves to show that they were spiritually poor, spiritually dull, and spiritual squanderers of grace.

We need to take great caution here. The decisions we make—for ourselves and in relation to God's commands—don't just have ramifications for ourselves. We are setting a course for our descendants. The decisions you and I make today will affect our children and grandchildren tomorrow.

We can easily draw the lines between parents who are addicts or abusers and children who become addicts or abusers. Many, if not most, abusers of spouses or children were themselves abused as children. Now, every person's sin is his own sin; we don't get to pass the buck. But the sin that indwells us can also be cultivated and trained by example in a sort of counter "discipleship."

We draw such lines rather easily. But we try not to draw others. Mom and Dad, if you are always arguing, if there is not evident love for each other or evident love of God in your relationship, guess what you're training your children for? You are setting a course for others to follow after you.

Men and women using pornography are cultivating dysfunction in their own relationships, which will seed dysfunction in whatever comes out of those relationships. Children of parents married to an unbelieving spouse are more likely to marry an unbelieving spouse themselves. The cycle continues.

The cycle of faithlessness is dangerous. Genesis 4 gives us a great caution for that.

But we also get hope. The story of everything has a very happy ending, and it is foreshadowed throughout all the little stories that make up the big story.

There is hope. It's laid out generationally in another branch of the family tree found in Genesis 4:

> And Adam knew his wife again, and she bore a son and called his name Seth, for she said, "God has appointed for me another offspring instead of Abel, for Cain killed him." To Seth also a son was born, and he called his name Enosh. At that time people began to call upon the name of the LORD. (vv. 25–26)

Seth becomes the replacement child for Abel. And out of Seth's line eventually comes Noah, who is the only man deemed righteous when God decides to bring his seventy-times-seven vengeance upon the earth full of Lamechites. And out of Noah's line comes Shem, the father of the Jewish people, whom God has chosen out of all the peoples to be his covenant people, out of which will come his incarnate Son, Jesus Christ.

Man, can God tell a story, or what?

We have the choice of what story to tell with our marriages, sex lives, and family life. We can tell one that exalts us, that makes us the center of the universe, or one that exalts God, that puts us in the position of leaning totally on God's sovereign grace. When we choose the latter storyline, we find that a legacy of faith is enduring.

Many of you reading this book are believers in Christ because of one believing parent or grandparent. Some of you are the only believer in your family. Some of you are saved because God used one person to step out in faith and share the gospel with you.

Some of us credit a strong culture of faith in our family because of a grandma who prayed constantly every day and had a well-worn Bible on her kitchen table.

The decisions you make have real-world consequences. This is why Proverbs 22:6 says, "Train up a child in the way he should go; even when he is old he will not depart from it." This isn't magic; it's not a guarantee. Every person is responsible for his own faith, just like each person is responsible for his own faithlessness. But it means that the course you set, the demeanor you set spiritually and theologically, can create a legacy of faith.

Ray Ortlund writes:

> I think about my dad a lot. I miss him so much it aches sometimes. But the most important thing he taught me was this. There is only one way to live: all-out, go-for-broke, risk-taking enthusiasm for Christ.
>
> Halfway Christianity is the most miserable existence of all. Halfhearted Christians know enough about their sin to feel guilty about themselves, but they haven't given themselves enough to the Savior to become happy in him. Wholehearted Christianity is happy.
>
> How could my dad get there and stay there? He really, really knew that God loved him and had completely forgiven all his sins at the cross of Jesus. He did not wring his hands, wondering what God thought of him. He believed the good news, his spirit soared and he could never do too much for Jesus.
>
> I am thankful for what I saw in my dad. It's the most valuable thing anyone has ever given me. I want everyone to have this treasure.[5]

I want my kids to be able to say that about me.

And yet I also know that how my kids turn out, what my legacy actually says about me and about God, is not ultimately up to me but up to God himself. God's grace is superior to family legacies.

Nobody goes to hell on their parents' sins. And nobody goes to heaven on their parents' faith. Nobody's getting to the pearly gates and hearing God say, "I knew your dad. He was a real piece of work." Or, "I knew your grandma. Sweet lady. Come on in."

This is good news, both ways, and here's why:

As sweet as your grandmother was, as wonderfully faithful as your mother was, and as fantastically spiritual as your dad was,

---

[5] Ray Ortlund, "The Most Important Thing My Dad Taught Me," *Christ Is Deeper Still* (blog), October 31, 2011, http://www.thegospelcoalition.org/blogs/rayortlund/2011/10/31/most-important -thing-my-dad-taught-me/.

they're all still sinners who cannot get into heaven on their own merits. They don't have enough righteousness for themselves, let alone you! So it's good you don't trust them.

It's also good news, of course, because as bad as anybody was in your family—and as bad as you may be yourself—there's no such thing as being too sinful for Christ Jesus to redeem. From Genesis 4 onward throughout the Old Testament, over and over again the people of God do stupid, sinful things. And over and over again God says, "You are mine. I am yours. Forever. You may be faithless but I will be faithful."

In Lamech's prideful claim to visit vengeance seventy-seven times, we see a foreshadow of that curious exchange between Peter and Jesus in Matthew 18 where Peter asks, "How many times do I need to forgive someone?" and Jesus says, "Seventy times seven."

Why? Because that's how forgiving Jesus himself is.

No matter your legacy, no matter your trajectory, no matter what your parents or grandparents put on you, no matter what your spouse has done to you or demands of you, no matter how terrible or detrimental or unfortunate your situation may be—you are not unsaveable. You are not unlovable. You are not unapprovable. You know the secret of the universe.

The gospel of God's grace is the great interrupter. It is the loophole to the law of legacy. God's grace is greater than all family trees. His Son is the vine, in which if we abide, we will have life abundant and bear much fruit.

This is also great news for those of you who can't have children, or who never get married (whether by choice or circumstances). Marriage is permanent, but it's not eternal. There is a better inheritance than family legacy. It is found in the treasure of Christ, in being joint-heirs with him in the eternal joy of his coming kingdom.

The Lord loves you. He is wooing you. He may be taking you into the wilderness for a time, but he does so to romance you (Hos. 2:14–15), to sweep you away and treat you with the finest and choicest pleasures beyond all attraction, beyond all relationships, beyond all ecstasies, which will by contrast seem the palest glows compared to the blazing flame of his holy righteousness sworn to you, guaranteed to you, and secured for you. He will in the gospel give those unsatisfied by marriage and sex a reward greater than any earthly legacy (Isa. 56:3–5).

> Then I heard what seemed to be the voice of a great multitude, like the roar of many waters and like the sound of mighty peals of thunder, crying out,
>
> Hallelujah!
> For the Lord our God
>   the Almighty reigns.
> Let us rejoice and exult
>   and give him the glory,
> for the marriage of the Lamb has come,
>   and his Bride has made herself ready;
> it was granted her to clothe herself
>   with fine linen, bright and pure. (Rev. 19:6–8)

OSAGE CITY PUBLIC LIBRARY
515 MAIN
OSAGE CITY, KS 66523

10

Body and Soul

God's Plan for You

So there I was, sitting in bumper-to-bumper traffic in Houston, Texas. The humidity was suffocating. But it was nothing compared to my own sense of aimlessness, of disconnection and insignificance. My heart had been searching the dial of the universe for quite some time, my own spiritual SETI program, but on that day, in that moment, I heard the loud ping. The Wow! signal came blaring through. "I don't think I belong here."

I looked around at the cars on the road. Some people seemed happy, sure, but most looked just as miserable as I did. Most had their music or talk radio turned up, perhaps to drown out that inner voice nagging them to take stock of their lives.

I looked around at the buildings on either side of the highway. Businesses of all kinds, office spaces. Full of people doing that day what they'd been doing every day for a very long time. Just trying to make a living, to carve out their own space in the world. The human condition of sin does not negate the nobility in the mandate all mankind keeps trying to follow—take dominion, fill the earth and subdue it. God gave us to the world, and he gave the world to

us for that reason. It's just that most of us are trying to take dominion for our own glory, and not for God's.

Now, suppose as I was sitting in that car, steaming in the hot
Houston air and stewing in my own spiritual malaise, an eighteen-
wheeler came barreling through the intersection across from me at
a high rate of speed, plowed over the median, and smashed into me.
The car would collapse into itself, and so would I.

If I was lucky, I would die quickly. My heart would be crushed
or my brain, and all my earthly longing, my sense of historical and
living disconnection would be gone. *Poof.* Just like that.

My family and my friends would grieve me for a long while. I'd
like to think I'd never be gotten over, but only those closest to me
would take a while to recover. Then they'd get to the point of missing me, but not grieving me. Then there would come days where
they'd be surprised that I didn't come to their mind at all.

For a few others who didn't know me, they may see a newspaper
notice or television report or even some eyewitness tweet or Facebook update about the incident. They wouldn't know my name,
necessarily, but only that I'd died in a terrible traffic accident.

Most everyone else in existence wouldn't even notice. They'd
have no way of knowing. My life with all its hopes and dreams
and ambitions and aspirations would simply vanish, like a vapor
warmed to nothing by the hot sun.

But my life would not be over. In a way, this would be only the
beginning.

The Appointment

My body's just been smashed to goo by an eighteen-wheeler. What
do I do now? I don't exist on the earthly plane. My body is there,
but my consciousness is not. What happens next?

Do I go toward the light?

What happens when you die?

First, we need to recognize that while for many people dying
comes as a complete surprise, our death is never a surprise to God.

You hear people saying, "He died too soon," or, "He was taken before his time." And even if we live to a ripe old age and die of "natural causes," we still don't know now how old we will be. We don't know the date and time of our death. It could be in one decade or several. It could be in one minute or one day. Proverbs 27:1 says, "Do not boast about tomorrow, for you do not know what a day may bring." The apostle James is even more blunt: "Yet you do not know what tomorrow will bring. What is your life? For you are a mist that appears for a little time and then vanishes" (James 4:14).

We are not promised tomorrow. So there's no way of telling. We simply don't know.

But the Author does.

"In your book," says Koheleth's dad, King David, "were written, every one of them, the days that were formed for me, when as yet there was none of them" (Ps. 139:16). The ageless Ancient of Days knows how many days we've got. But he doesn't just know our days; he's written them. He's created them. He's the one who declares the end from the beginning (Isa. 46:10).

So the exact second of our deaths is known by God and even set by him. He has already made the appointment for us. We don't know when this appointment is, but we can know for sure that it will come neither early nor late. It will come precisely when God has planned it. "It is appointed for man to die once," Hebrews 9:27 says. And there you have it.

So we're all going to die. (Well, unless you're a believer in Christ who is alive when he returns, but we'll get to that in a second.) None of us gets out of here alive.

Where does the story go after death? Most people think their story ends there. Maybe somehow it lives on in the memories of their loved ones. But their own personal story, they assume, concludes when their body stops working. But if we could really grasp how long eternity is, we'd never confuse this earthly life for the summation of our life story.

The appointed time comes. "After that," Hebrews 9:27 goes on to say, "comes judgment."

When you die, you don't cease to exist. In fact, your truest self is revealed. You can call that your soul or your spirit or what-have-you. But the real you, the essential you, is still functioning, still feeling. And the Author says in his inspired Book that we must then stand before him and give an account.

The only true fork in the spiritual road appears here. Before this moment, the only way we might agree that all paths lead to the same place is if we agree that place is the judgment seat of Christ (2 Cor. 5:10). But from there, there are only two destinations: eternal joy with Christ or eternal torment apart from him (Matt. 25:31–46).

For those who have believed in God's true story by placing their faith in Jesus Christ for the forgiveness of sins and the gift of eternal life, to be absent from the body is to be present with the Lord (2 Cor. 5:8). For those who do not know Jesus as Lord and Savior, who have trusted in themselves, whether they're religious or not, the only thing that awaits is the only reward possible for self-righteousness—the place called hell (Luke 12:5).

This is the appointment awaiting us all. Many want to avoid it. But God will keep it, which means you will too.

Life and Death after Life and Death

The story continues. For those found at this appointed time clothed in the righteousness of Christ—meaning, they have placed their faith in Jesus's perfect obedience, sacrificial death, and glorious resurrection for their salvation—they will pass that test of judgment into the joys of heaven, the spiritual place where the triune God lives in all his visible, manifest splendor. The ancients often called this paradise or "Abraham's bosom." The angels are there. The saints that have passed before us are there. There are even some there in physical bodies that were assumed up into heaven—Enoch, for example, and Elijah. And let's not forget the resurrected, glorified Jesus Christ, the best part of heaven, the one without which heaven would not be heaven.

Jesus promises his disciples:

> In my Father's house are many rooms. If it were not so, would I have told you that I go to prepare a place for you? And if I go and prepare a place for you, I will come again and will take you to myself, that where I am you may be also. (John 14:2–3)

But heaven is just the beginning for the saint of God. Those who die go to heaven as an "intermediate state," a sort of spiritual holding plane until the appointed time when Christ will return to earth again (called the *second coming*), rescue his living saints, finally conquer evil and vanquish death, and usher in the new heavens and the new earth. What happens to both the saints in heaven and the saints still alive on earth at that time is the real wonder of "life after death." It is life *after* life after death. Paul explains:

> For as in Adam all die, so also in Christ shall all be made alive. But each in his own order: Christ the firstfruits, then at his coming those who belong to Christ. Then comes the end, when he delivers the kingdom to God the Father after destroying every rule and every authority and power
> . . . Behold! I tell you a mystery. We shall not all sleep, but we shall all be changed, in a moment, in the twinkling of an eye, at the last trumpet. For the trumpet will sound, and the dead will be raised imperishable, and we shall be changed. For this perishable body must put on the imperishable, and this mortal body must put on immortality. (1 Cor. 15:22–24, 51–53)

Every Christian then will receive his resurrection body—an immortal, glory-powered version of their present and past body—with which to see Jesus, worship Jesus, and enjoy Jesus. And, we assume, to frolic freely upon the renewed creation, to work and play and love and enjoy every good thing, only this time without fear, without worry, without sin, without corruption, without injustice, and without death. The shalom of creation before the fall, that "it is good"-ness will be restored, but even more so. The new heavens and the new earth will be better than Eden. This was God's plan all along.

For those who have not trusted Christ, the story goes on, as well, but to a never-ending ending. Hell is not only as bad as you feared it might be—it is actually worse. We have some idea based on various scriptural evidence that there may be degrees of punishment in hell just as there appear to be some degrees of reward in heaven, but please know that the "best" of hell will still be worse than anything a sinner could imagine. The Bible speaks of hell as both dark and fiery, as both a place of torment by God's wrath and a place of utter isolation and separation. And every indication we have in the Bible is that this punishment goes on forever. For all eternity.

And when Christ returns to drench all creation with his glory, the outcome for those who have not trusted him, whether departed in hell or alive and being reserved for it in the future, will be to find themselves thrown into what John describes as a lake of fire:

> Then Death and Hades were thrown into the lake of fire. This is the second death, the lake of fire. And if anyone's name was not found written in the book of life, he was thrown into the lake of fire. (Rev. 20:14–15)

Another death after death, the second death.

Best believe that God is going to put everything back to rights. He will not let sin have the last word. God's characters cannot ruin or rule the story. From eternity past, in his infinite creative mind, he determined to bring his glory to bear by allowing the fall that he might redeem sinners and restore creation. This way we know more of his glory than if he'd chosen some other narrative variation.

> So teach us to number our days that we may get a heart of wisdom. (Ps. 90:12)

Until we get that heart of wisdom, we will never "number our days" with that final appointment in mind. We will keep scanning the dial of the world looking for connection and significance. We will miss the Wow! signal of the gospel.

We are all winding down and dying. But the story of everything tells us that Christ is the cure for everything. At every point since the fall, he is bringing redemption, freedom, salvation, and restoration.

Where our sin brings pain and toil, Christ comes to give us a burden that is easy and a yoke that is light. And when he consummates his kingdom, the pain and toil of cursed creation will be gone. He will wipe away every tear.

Where our sin brings division between mankind, Christ comes uniting us. In Christ (Gal. 3:28 tells us) there is no male or female, Jew or Greek, slave or free, but Christ is in all. He has given us the ministry of reconciliation (2 Cor. 5:18). He builds the church out of every tongue, tribe, race, and nation.

Where our sin brings spiritual bondage and spiritual warfare, Christ conquers sin and death and makes a mockery of the powers and principalities, putting them to open shame by triumphing over them in the cross. Consequently and concurrently, he binds the strong man that his brothers and sisters may plunder his goods, giving us power over the Serpent himself and the Serpent's demons by the blood of his own sacrifice. So that Paul can say in Romans 16:20, "The God of peace will soon crush Satan under your feet."

Where our sin brings subjection, cursedness, and groaning to creation itself, Christ brings a restoration. "Behold, I am making all things new," Christ says (not all new things!), so that Paul says in Romans 8 that creation is groaning not in death pangs but *birth* pangs, as it gives way to something better in its renewal. Christ ushers in the new heavens and the new earth, where shalom will be reinstituted at his return.

Where our sin brings death, Christ gives life and life abundant. Belief in him is credited to us as his righteousness, and when we are united to Christ, our bodies will pass away, but because of his saving death, our souls will pass into everlasting day, and because of his resurrection, we will receive glorified, immortal bodies to live forever in the new heavens and new earth after our own resurrection.

And where our sin divides us from God, Christ becomes our advocate, our mediator, our atoning and propitiating sacrifice, so that the God who owes us wrath now is reconciled to us and we become his beloved children. Where once we were cast out into exile, "Let us [now] with confidence," Hebrews 4:16 says, "draw near to the throne of grace, that we may receive mercy and find grace to help in time of need."

How Do You Want Your Story to End?

The story of everything is a true story. It is actually happening. And while history appears to be creeping along, the spiritual timing is not slow at all. He is actually coming soon (Rev. 3:11). Therefore, you should not put off your thinking about these things for another day, not even for another second. "Today, if you hear his voice, do not harden your hearts as in the rebellion" (Heb. 3:15).

How do you want your story to end?

Are you writing your own tale of epic you-ness? Put your pen down! Wave the white flag.

Scotty Smith says, "To believe the gospel is to stop giving God bit parts in our story, and to begin celebrating our place in His story."[1]

There's no better time than right this very second. "Behold, now is the favorable time; behold, now is the day of salvation" (2 Cor. 6:2).

I once shared this story of everything with a fellow who visited our church—we'll call him Derek—and what he said in his response was both incredibly impressive and incredibly depressing. He basically said he thought the secret to life was "living his best life now." He just wanted to leave the world a little better than

[1] Scotty Smith, Twitter post, November 14, 2014, 6:35 a.m., https://twitter.com/scottywardsmith/status/533221567149645824.

he found it. He wanted to do his best and be kind to others and make sure his memory was a warm one and an enduring one and an inspiring one.

But the problem with this is that it only goes for a little while. Derek's friends and family will remember him, just like mine would have remembered me if I'd been smashed to smithereens by that eighteen-wheeler. But eventually the memory will die too. Because the people who remember us will die. And maybe they've passed on some information about us. Maybe our grandkids know us or know about us. But what about their kids? What about our grandchildren's grandchildren? We'll at some point become just a line of data on a family tree.

"Well, you don't know about me!" you might say. "I'm a seriously memorable person. History will tell my tale for years to come."

All right.

Look, even if you do happen to be one of the rare few whose memory is likely to carry on for many years after death—like Moses or Madame Curie or Marlene Dietrich—the world is going to end someday, and then what will you have accomplished? Your record of audacious nobility and ambitious renown will be remembered by nobody, recorded nowhere. It will have become something infinitesimally tinier than even a speck of dust floating in the silent void of the endless abyss of space. If eternity is a line, world history is just a dot on that line, smaller than a grain of sand lying in the shadow of the Matterhorn. The Matterhorn is just a speck of sand on that line.

Even if you "change the world," in a million years, it won't matter, if God's story of everything isn't true.

But if God's story is true, what you do here has profound implications on what comes next. Or, rather, what comes next has profound implications on what you do here. Preparing for what comes next is, then, the most important thing you can do—beyond recycling, beyond saving for retirement, beyond saving the whales or the icebergs or the ozone layer, beyond getting the right people elected.

Jesus is indeed making all things new. The purpose of life now is to live in such a way that everything we do with everything points to his remaking of everything.

So, again: How do you want your story to end?

Let's go back to the beginning, once again. Let's see the conclusion there. The good news of Jesus Christ is embedded in Genesis 1 and 2 like the Fibonacci numbers are embedded in a seashell. Let's hold it up to our ear. Maybe we will hear the roaring waves of redemption in it.

Genesis 1 is certainly what Paul has in mind when he says in 2 Corinthians 4:6:

> For God, who said, "Let light shine out of darkness," has shone in our hearts to give the light of the knowledge of the glory of God in the face of Jesus Christ.

When God says in Genesis 1:3, "Let there be light," this is a foreshadowing of the light that shines into our hearts, Paul says, to reveal the saving glory of Christ to us. The light *is* the saving glory of Christ.

Like the great verse from the Charles Wesley hymn "And Can It Be" expresses:

> Long my imprisoned spirit lay,
> fast bound in sin and nature's night;
> thine eye diffused a quickening ray;
> I woke, the dungeon flamed with light;
> my chains fell off, my heart was free,
> I rose, went forth, and followed thee.

So Paul will say in 2 Corinthians 5:17 of those who have trusted in Jesus for the forgiveness of sins and the gift of eternal life, "If anyone is in Christ, he is a new creation."

Genesis 1 in fact lays the groundwork for the new creation work of salvation. Step by step it foreshadows the work God does in and through us by the power of the gospel. So now that we know the secret of the universe, the true and Spirit-proved theory of everything, let's look through it to read that first signal from outer space, reading Genesis 1 like this:

In the beginning, God created my body and mind.

But my heart was without form and void, and darkness was over my soul. And the Spirit of God was hovering over my way and hounding me.

And God said, "Let there be light," and a divine and supernatural light was imparted to me, illuminating my senses with his glory to behold his glory. And God breathed his Spirit into me and gave me life.

God separated the light from the darkness and brought me into everlasting day.

And God said, "Let there be separation of your life from chaos and death," and he placed my feet on the solid rock foundation of his promised-land kingdom.

And God said, "Come out from their midst and be separate." And it was so. God made me holy. And God saw that I was now good by his own decree.

And God said, "Let your heart sprout vegetation, plants yielding seed, the spiritual fruit of love, joy, peace, patience, kindness, goodness, faithfulness, gentleness, and self-control." And it was so.

And God said, "Let there be many more of these carriers of my light in the expanse of creation to proclaim the good news of the Light into the night. And let them be for signs and for seasons, and for days and years, and let them be lights in the expanse of the heavens to give light upon the earth." And it was so.

And God said, "Let the waters be full of fishers of men and let my Spirit descend like a dove to lead them into all truth." And God blessed them, saying, "Be fruitful and multiply and fill the furthest reaches of the earth with worshipers of God."

And God had remade us in the image of his Son. And he gave us dominion over demons and the kingdom of hell and promised us the inheritance of the new creation to come.

And God blessed us. And God said to us, "Be fruitful and multiply and fill the earth and subdue it."

And God said to us, "It is not good for you to be alone." So he made out of men the church, the body of Christ, that we might help her and she us. And for this reason a man will leave his independence and self-sovereignty and cleave to his new humanity.

And God saw that it was good.

Not The End.

Introduction

And so we end with a new beginning.

We are looking forward to the new heavens and the new earth. The key is to figure out how to live, by God's modus operandi (grace), in this earth under heaven in light of that one. So what do we make of everything? Is God going to renew it?

"Wait a minute," you're saying. "You promised the story of everything. You didn't mention a lot of stuff."

I'm not sure what I left out, but I am hearing your objection. I'll try to make up for some disappointment now. Is God going to remake . . .

Coffee? Yes.

Sports? Yes.

Movies? Sure.

Music? Of course.

Comic books? I think so.

Circuses? Yes, all right.

Tex-Mex? I can't imagine how it could get better, but yes.

Chocolate? Darn tootin'.

Quinoa? No, I think this will become bacon.

Cats? See *quinoa*, above.

But dogs and the Swiss Alps and everything in between? A thousand times yes.

Look, God is telling a great story, and it accounts for literally everything. There is no square inch under heaven or above it about which God does not say, "Mine."

So your search for connection and significance, the deepest cries of every human heart, must be found by tuning into this good news story. It is what makes sense of your life.

We must now see everything as ripe with meaning, full of God-glorifying potential.

Anthony Hoekema writes:

> As citizens of God's kingdom, we may not just write off the present earth as a total loss, or rejoice in its deterioration. We must indeed be working for a better world now. Our efforts to bring the kingdom of Christ into fuller manifestation are of eternal significance. . . . As we live on this earth, we are preparing for life on God's new earth. Through our kingdom service the building materials for that new earth are now being gathered. Bibles are being translated, peoples are being evangelized, believers are being renewed, and cultures are being transformed. Only eternity will reveal the full significance of what has been done for Christ here.[1]

He is making all things new. And he commands us to behold him doing it.

Can you imagine it? This is the beginning of the great story that awaits us at the end of this short chapter in history. We don't have all the answers; we don't see the vision perfectly. But through it we see the promise that is sure, the promise that gives us hope, the promise that answers the questions beneath our questions and helps us make sense of the chaotic, unstable world around us. Tim Keller says:

> Christians do not claim that their faith gives them omniscience or absolute knowledge of reality. Only God has that. But they believe that the Christian account of things—creation, fall, redemption, and restoration—makes the most sense of the world. I ask you to put on Christianity like a pair of spectacles and look at the world with it. See what power it has to explain what we know and see.[2]

---

[1] Anthony A. Hoekema, *The Bible and the Future* (Grand Rapids, MI: Eerdmans, 1994), 287.
[2] Timothy Keller, *The Reason for God: Belief in an Age of Skepticism* (New York: Riverhead, 2009), 127.

Or as C. S. Lewis says, "I believe in Christianity as I believe that the Sun has risen, not only because I see it, but because by it I see everything else."[3]

So let's walk around our world with the story's promise of newness in mind. Let's fix in our imaginations the visionary promise of the new heavens and the new earth, of that day when the space where God lives comes reigning down into our world with visible, tangible, final results. Let's see the darkness fleeing. Let's see the tears drying up, the stooped backs straightened, the dry and weary ground refreshed with living water and living abundance. Sin will be vanquished. Injustice will be judged. Death will be swallowed up into the void forever. And the King of Glory will be enthroned over the earth. His glory will gleam like diamonds off the redeemed skyscrapers of New York City and Tokyo. His glory will beam with the brightest whiteness off the renewed Swiss Alps. His glory will dance and sparkle off the crashing waves of the ocean shores and illuminate the deepest ocean trenches. We will wince no more, worry no more, war no more. We will wonder. Forever and ever.

---

[3] C. S. Lewis, "Is Theology Poetry?," in *"The Weight of Glory" and Other Addresses* (New York: HarperCollins, 2001), 140.

General Index

Scripture Index

Also Available from Jared C. Wilson

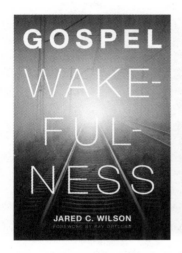

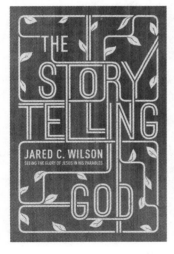

For more information, visit crossway.org.